Decoding the TOEFL® iBT

Advanced

WRITING

INTRODUCTION

For many learners of English, the TOEFL® iBT will be the most important standardized test they ever take. Unfortunately for a large number of these individuals, the material covered on the TOEFL® iBT remains a mystery to them, so they are unable to do well on the test. We hope that by using the *Decoding the TOEFL® iBT* series, individuals who take the TOEFL® iBT will be able to excel on the test and, in the process of using the book, may unravel the mysteries of the test and therefore make the material covered on the TOEFL® iBT more familiar to themselves.

The TOEFL® iBT covers the four main skills that a person must learn when studying any foreign language: reading, listening, speaking, and writing. The *Decoding the TOEFL® iBT* series contains books that cover all four of these skills. The *Decoding the TOEFL® iBT* series contains books with three separate levels for all four of the topics as well as the *Decoding the TOEFL® iBT Actual Test* books. These books are all designed to enable learners to utilize them to become better prepared to take the TOEFL® iBT. This book, *Decoding the TOEFL® iBT Writing Advanced*, covers the writing aspect of the test. It is designed to help learners prepare for the Writing section of the TOEFL® iBT.

Decoding the TOEFL® iBT Writing Advanced can be used by learners who are taking classes and also by individuals who are studying by themselves. It contains two parts, each of which contains ten chapters. Part A covers the Integrated Writing Task while Part B covers the Independent Writing Task. There is also one actual test at the end of the book. Each chapter has either two Integrated tasks or two Independent questions. It also contains exercises designed to help learners understand how to write the best possible essays for the Writing section. The passages and questions in *Decoding the TOEFL® iBT Writing Advanced* are lower levels than those found on the TOEFL® iBT. Individuals who use *Decoding the TOEFL® iBT Writing Advanced* will therefore be able to prepare themselves not only to take the TOEFL® iBT but also to perform well on the test.

We hope that everyone who uses *Decoding the TOEFL® iBT Writing Advanced* will be able to become more familiar with the TOEFL® iBT and will additionally improve his or her score on the test. As the title of the book implies, we hope that learners can use it to crack the code on the TOEFL® iBT, to make the test itself less mysterious and confusing, and to get the highest grade possible. Finally, we hope that both learners and instructors can use this book to its full potential. We wish all of you the best of luck as you study English and prepare for the TOEFL® iBT, and we hope that *Decoding the TOEFL® iBT Writing Advanced* can provide you with assistance during the course of your studies.

Michael A. Putlack
Stephen Poirier

TABLE
OF
CONTENTS

ABOUT THE TOEFL® iBT WRITING SECTION

How the Section Is Organized

The writing section is the last part of the TOEFL® iBT and consists of two portions: the Integrated Writing Task and the Independent Writing Task. The Integrated Writing Task requires test takers to explain how a short reading passage and lecture are related while the Independent Writing Task requires test takers to explain their opinions about a given situation. Test takers have 20 minutes to complete the Integrated Writing Task. For the Independent Writing Task, they have 30 minutes.

The writing section tests the ability of test takers to organize information clearly. The responses do not have to be creative or original. They just need to be succinct and direct. The most important thing test takers can do to boost their score is to present their ideas clearly by using relevant examples. Strong support and vivid details are essential for earning a top score.

Changes in the Writing Section

There are no major changes in the Writing section. However, in the Independent Writing Task, the directions tend to be longer than before on average. The question also often asks not only about a general opinion but also about a specific situation. This can be seen as a measure to prevent test takers from writing memorized essays. At the end of the question, there are directions that prohibit the writing of a memorized example. Therefore, it is important that test takers practice writing essays based on their own ideas instead of trying to memorize model essays.

Question Types

TYPE 1 The Integrated Writing Task

The Integrated Writing Task consists of three parts. Test takers begin by reading a passage approximately 230 to 300 words in length for 3 minutes. Following this, test takers listen to a lecture that either supports or contradicts the reading. Finally, test takers are given 20 minutes to write their essays. The essays should be between 150 and 225 words in length. During this time, the reading passage will reappear on the computer screen. Again, it is important to remember that test takers are not expected to present any new ideas in their essays. Instead, test takers must summarize the lecture and explain its relationship with the reading passage by providing examples from both.

ABOUT THE
TOEFL® iBT
WRITING SECTION

There are five possible writing tasks test takers will be presented with, but they all require test takers to summarize the lecture and to explain how it either supports or contradicts the reading.

If the listening passage challenges or contradicts the reading passage, the tasks will be presented in one of the following ways:

- Summarize the points made in the lecture, being sure to explain how they cast doubt on specific points made in the reading passage.

  cf. This question type accounts for most of the questions that have been asked on the TOEFL® iBT so far.

- Summarize the points made in the lecture, being sure to explain how they challenge specific claims/arguments made in the reading passage.

- Summarize the points made in the lecture, being sure to specifically explain how they answer the problems raised in the reading passage.

If the listening passage supports or strengthens the reading passage, the tasks will be presented in one of the following ways:

- Summarize the points made in the lecture, being sure to specifically explain how they support the explanations in the reading passage.

- Summarize the points made in the lecture, being sure to specifically explain how they strengthen specific points made in the reading passage.

TYPE 2 The Independent Writing Task

The Independent Writing Task is the second half of the TOEFL® iBT writing section. Test takers have 30 minutes to write an essay explaining their options about a given question. Typically, an effective response is between 300 and 400 words in length. In order to earn a top score, test takers must clearly present their ideas by using logical arguments and effective supporting examples. Strong responses generally include an introductory paragraph with a clear thesis statement, two or three supporting paragraphs with focused topic sentences, and a brief concluding paragraph.

There are three possible writing tasks you will be presented with, but they all ask you to express your opinion about an important issue.

For the agree/disagree type, the task will be presented in the following way:

- Do you agree or disagree with the following statement?
  [A sentence or sentences that present an issue]
  Use specific reasons and examples to support your answer.
  cf. This question type accounts for most of the essay topics that have been asked on the TOEFL® iBT so far.

For the preference type, the task will be presented in the following way:

- Some people prefer X. Others prefer Y. Which do you prefer? Use specific reasons and examples to support your choice.

For the opinion type, the task will be presented in the following way:

- [A sentence or sentences that state a fact]
  In your opinion, what is one thing that should be . . . ? Use specific reasons and examples to support your answer.

HOW TO USE THIS BOOK

Decoding the TOEFL® iBT Writing Advanced is designed to be used either as a textbook in a classroom environment or as a study guide for individual learners. There are 2 parts with 10 chapters each in this book. Each chapter provides 2 sample tasks or questions. There are 4 or 5 sections in each chapter, which enable you to build up your skills on a particular writing task. At the end of the book, there is one actual test of the Writing section of the TOEFL® iBT.

Part A Integrated Writing Task

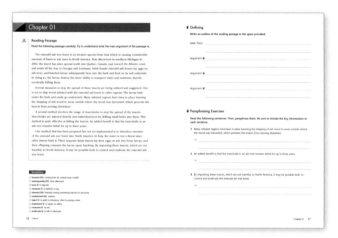

A | Reading Passage

This section contains a reading passage between 230 and 300 words long. There is a vocabulary section with definitions of difficult words or phrases in the passage. There are also sections for outlining and paraphrasing to make sure you understand the material you read and can condense it.

B | Listening Lecture

This section contains a listening lecture between 230 and 300 words long. There is a section for note-taking so that you can write down the key information you hear in the lecture. There is also a paraphrasing section to make sure you can condense the information that you heard.

C | Combining the Main Points

This section contains 3 excerpts each from the reading passage and listening lecture. You should read the excerpts and then use the information in them to complete each sentence. Then, complete the sample essay on the next page by using the outline you wrote and the notes you took.

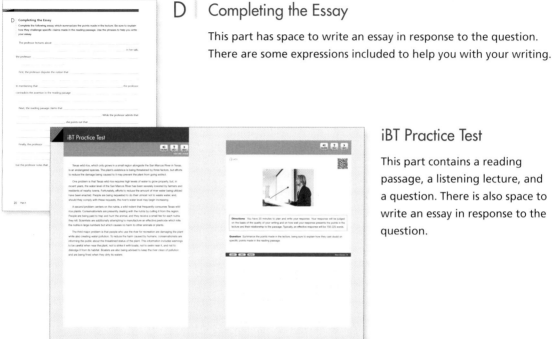

D | Completing the Essay

This part has space to write an essay in response to the question. There are some expressions included to help you with your writing.

iBT Practice Test

This part contains a reading passage, a listening lecture, and a question. There is also space to write an essay in response to the question.

Independent Writing Task

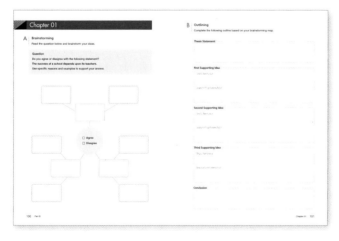

A | Brainstorming

This section contains a question and space for brainstorming to prepare to write your answer.

B | Outlining

This part has space for an outline that will describe what information will be included in the introduction, body, and conclusion of the essay.

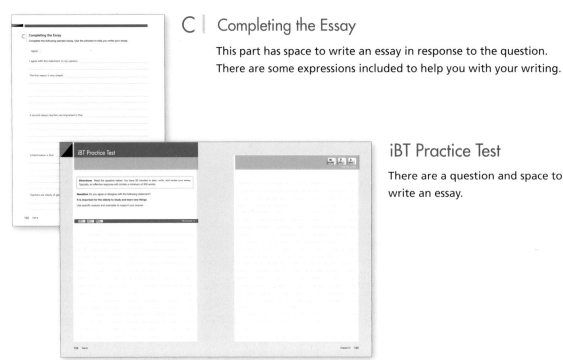

C | Completing the Essay

This part has space to write an essay in response to the question. There are some expressions included to help you with your writing.

iBT Practice Test

There are a question and space to write an essay.

● **Actual Test** (at the end of the book)

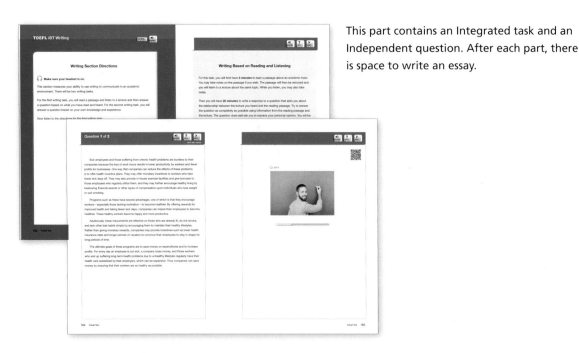

This part contains an Integrated task and an Independent question. After each part, there is space to write an essay.

Part A

Integrated Writing Task

Integrated Writing Task

◢ About the Question

The Integrated Writing Task contains three parts. The first part is a reading passage that is around 230 to 300 words long. You are given 3 minutes to read the passage. Next, you will hear a lecture that either supports the reading passage or goes against it in some manner. Last, you will be given 20 minutes to write an essay on the reading passage and listening lecture. Your essay should be 150 to 225 words long. While you are writing your essay, you will be able to see the reading passage on the screen. To write your essay, simply provide a summary of the lecture and explain how it is connected to the reading passage. You should be sure to use the examples that are provided in the two passages. However, avoid using any new ideas or examples that do not appear in either of the passages. Your essay must be taken solely from the information presented in the two passages.

There are five possible writing tasks that may be presented to you. All of them require that you summarize the lecture and explain how it supports or goes against the reading passage. The vast majority of passages have the lecture contradicting, casting doubt on, or challenging the issues that are mentioned in the reading passage. Very few lectures support the reading passage.

If the listening passage challenges or contradicts the reading passage, the tasks will be presented in one of the following ways:

- Summarize the points made in the lecture, being sure to explain how they cast doubt on specific points made in the reading.

  cf. This question type accounts for most of the questions that have been asked on the TOEFL® iBT so far.

- Summarize the points made in the lecture, being sure to explain how they challenge specific claims/arguments made in the reading.

- Summarize the points made in the lecture, being sure to specifically explain how they answer the problems raised in the reading passage.

If the listening passage supports or strengthens the reading passage, the tasks will be presented in one of the following ways:

- Summarize the points made in the lecture, being sure to specifically explain how they support the explanations in the reading passage.

- Summarize the points made in the lecture, being sure to specifically explain how they strengthen specific points made in the reading passage.

Sample Question

In recent years, companies have begun recruiting employees by offering signing bonuses. These cash payments, which can amount to several thousand dollars—or even tens of thousands of dollars—are highly effective for several reasons.

One is that bonuses can induce the best applicants to sign with the firms offering them cash. These days, many companies offer similar payment and benefits packages to potential employees and have nearly identical working conditions, too. This is especially true of companies located in the same cities or regions. Since the compensation and working conditions differ so little, the best applicants are typically persuaded by the sizes of the signing bonuses they are offered.

Another benefit is that signing bonuses can provide new workers with the financial assistance they require to live in certain areas. In the United States, New York, Boston, San Francisco, and other large metropolises have extremely high costs of living. A large signing bonus can tremendously help people be able to afford the high prices in those places until they receive their first few paychecks. Recent college graduates in particular are attracted to these bonuses since they may have little or no savings and thus have difficulty transitioning to expensive urban locations.

Finally, large signing bonuses can indicate just how much companies value individuals and want to hire them. Workers tend to be impressed with companies that offer them huge sums of money simply to work at them. Not only is the money appreciated, but the workers also realize that the companies are making significant financial investments in them. As such, these employers are likely to provide their new employees with the training and additional support they require to excel at their positions. Knowing that their careers will be assisted, the applicants accept these employment offers and bonuses.

A00

| Script | **M Professor:** Many of you are seniors, so you're likely searching for jobs for after graduation. In the next few months, a few of you might be offered signing bonuses by some firms. Sounds great, doesn't it . . . ? You get paid merely to sign your name to a contract. Well, it's a good deal for workers, but companies don't always benefit.

One reason is that numerous employees accept the money but later quit working once they can. In general, employees receiving signing bonuses are contractually obligated to work for a certain period of time. Depending on the size of the bonus, this could be a few months or a couple of years. After all, um, companies want to receive positive returns on their investments. Nevertheless, I've seen many people take the money, put in the required time at their companies, and then resign and depart for other firms as soon as they're legally permitted to do so.

Here's something else . . . Companies giving out signing bonuses are frequently located in metropolitan areas, which are quite expensive. Well, signing bonuses help workers get by at first, but what happens when the workers spend all that money . . . ? They have to survive on their salaries, which might not be sufficient. These employees often become disappointed with their salaries and demand more money while others quit and move elsewhere. Either way, the companies lose.

A final point is that bonuses make employees focus almost exclusively on earning money, which essentially transforms them into, uh, into mercenaries. Of course, uh, everyone works for money, but companies want people who are interested in their jobs and actually enjoy working. Those individuals who are lured by signing bonuses frequently don't care about their jobs but are only interested in the sizes of the checks they're getting.

Directions You have 20 minutes to plan and write your response. Your response will be judged on the basis of the quality of your writing and on how well your response presents the points in the lecture and their relationship to the passage. Typically, an effective response will be 150-225 words.

Question Summarize the points made in the lecture, being sure to explain how they challenge specific claims made in the reading passage.

Sample Essay

Both the lecture and the reading passage are about signing bonuses which companies use to convince job applicants to accept job offers. While the author of the reading passage believes the signing bonuses are effective, the professor finds fault with them.

The first point the professor makes is that many individuals accept signing bonuses but only stay at their firms for short amounts of time. By pointing out how these people cause companies to receive poor returns on their investments, the professor challenges the claim in the reading passage that companies can get top applicants to work for them.

A second problem the professor mentions is that the people receiving signing bonuses often live in expensive metropolises. After spending their bonus money, they cannot afford to live there, so they either demand higher salaries or quit their jobs. This goes against the argument in the reading passage that employees such as recent college graduates can use their bonuses to be able to live in costly regions.

The last point the professor discusses is how much employees who receive bonuses become interested in making money. Although the author of the reading passage thinks these individuals will appreciate the support their companies are providing them, the professor disagrees. He feels that they will only think about money and will not care much about their jobs.

Chapter 01

A Reading Passage

Read the following passage carefully. Try to understand what the main argument of the passage is.

The emerald ash tree borer is an invasive species from Asia which is causing considerable amounts of harm to ash trees in North America. First discovered in southern Michigan in 2002, the insect has since spread north into Quebec, Canada, east toward the Atlantic coast, and south all the way to Georgia and Louisiana. Adult female emerald ash borers lay eggs on ash trees, and hatched larvae subsequently bore into the bark and feed on its soft underside. In doing so, the larvae destroy the trees' ability to transport water and nutrients, thereby eventually killing them.

Several measures to stop the spread of these insects are being utilized and suggested. One is not to ship wood infested with the emerald ash borer to other regions. The larvae hide under the bark and easily go undetected. Many infested regions have laws in place banning the shipping of ash wood to areas outside where the wood was harvested, which prevents the insects from moving elsewhere.

A second method involves the usage of insecticides to stop the spread of the insects. Insecticides are injected directly into individual trees by drilling small holes into them. This method is quite effective at killing the insects. An added benefit is that the insecticide in an ash tree remains lethal for up to three years.

One method that has been proposed but not yet implemented is to introduce enemies of the emerald ash tree borer into North America. In Asia, the insect is not a threat since other insects hunt it. Three separate Asian insects lay their eggs on ash tree borer larvae, and their offspring consume the larvae upon hatching. By importing these insects, which are not harmful, to North America, it may be possible both to control and eradicate the emerald ash tree borer.

Vocabulary

- **invasive** *adj* coming from an outside area; hostile
- **subsequently** *adv* next; afterward
- **bore** *v* to dig into
- **measure** *n* a method; a way
- **infested** *adj* infected; having something harmful or annoying
- **undetected** *adj* unseen
- **inject** *v* to add; to introduce, often by giving a shot
- **implement** *v* to apply; to utilize
- **consume** *v* to eat
- **eradicate** *v* to kill; to eliminate

Outlining

Write an outline of the reading passage in the space provided.

Main Point

Argument ❶

Argument ❷

Argument ❸

Paraphrasing Exercises

Read the following sentences. Then, paraphrase them. Be sure to include the key information in each sentence.

1 Many infested regions have laws in place banning the shipping of ash wood to areas outside where the wood was harvested, which prevents the insects from moving elsewhere.

→

2 An added benefit is that the insecticide in an ash tree remains lethal for up to three years.

→

3 By importing these insects, which are not harmful, to North America, it may be possible both to control and eradicate the emerald ash tree borer.

→

B | Listening Lecture 🎧 A01

Listen to a lecture on the topic you just read about. Be sure to take notes while you listen.

◢ Note-Taking

Main Point _____

_____

Argument ❶ _____

_____

Argument ❷ _____

_____

Argument ❸ _____

_____

◢ Paraphrasing Exercises

Read the following sentences. Then, paraphrase them. Be sure to include the key information in each sentence.

1 Lately, the government has been attempting to halt the spread of the insect by banning ash wood from being shipped even as firewood.

→ _____

_____

2 Using insecticides would require excessive manpower and money, so it's not a practical option.

→ _____

_____

3 People say these other insects are harmless, yet we simply can't anticipate what damage a new species can do when it's introduced into an environment where it has no natural enemies.

→ _____

_____

C Combining the Main Points

Read the following sentences from the reading passage and listening lecture. Then, combine each pair of sentences by using the given patterns.

1 **Reading** Many infested regions have laws in place banning the shipping of ash wood to areas outside where the wood was harvested, which prevents the insects from moving elsewhere.

Listening You see, the insect has wings and can fly. So flying from place to place is one of the ways the emerald ash borer has been spreading. Halting log shipments simply won't work.

→ **In mentioning that** _____ **the**

professor contradicts the assertion in the reading passage that _____

_____

2 **Reading** Insecticides are injected directly into individual trees by drilling small holes into them. This method is quite effective at killing the insects. An added benefit is that the insecticide in an ash tree remains lethal for up to three years.

Listening Sure, you can use insecticides on the ash trees in your yard, but what about when there are tens of thousands of ash trees in a single forest . . . ? Using insecticides would require excessive manpower and money, so it's not a practical option.

→ **The reading passage claims that** _____

_____ **. While the professor admits that** _____

she points out that _____

3 **Reading** Three separate Asian insects lay their eggs on ash tree borer larvae, and their offspring consume the larvae upon hatching. By importing these insects, which are not harmful, to North America, it may be possible both to control and eradicate the emerald ash tree borer.

Listening Who knows what harm they could cause? Sure, people say these other insects are harmless, yet we simply can't anticipate what damage a new species can do when it's introduced into an environment where it has no natural enemies.

→ **The author of the reading passage argues** _____

_____ **, but the professor notes**

that _____

D | Completing the Essay

Complete the following essay which summarizes the points made in the lecture. Be sure to explain how they challenge specific claims made in the reading passage. Use the phrases to help you write your essay.

The professor lectures about _____

_____. In her talk,

the professor _____

_____.

First, the professor disputes the notion that _____

_____.

In mentioning that _____, the professor

contradicts the assertion in the reading passage _____

_____.

Next, the reading passage claims that _____

_____. While the professor admits that

_____, she points out that _____

_____

_____.

Finally, the professor _____

_____. The author of the reading passage argues that

_____,

but the professor notes that _____.

Texas wild rice, which only grows in a small region alongside the San Marcos River in Texas, is an endangered species. The plant's existence is being threatened by three factors, but efforts to reduce the damage being caused to it may prevent the plant from going extinct.

One problem is that Texas wild rice requires high levels of water to grow properly, but, in recent years, the water level of the San Marcos River has been severely lowered by farmers and residents of nearby towns. Fortunately, efforts to reduce the amount of river water being utilized have been enacted. People are being requested to do their utmost not to waste water, and, should they comply with these requests, the river's water level may begin increasing.

A second problem centers on the nutria, a wild rodent that frequently consumes Texas wild rice plants. Conservationists are presently dealing with the nutria by culling it from the region. People are being paid to trap and hunt the animal, and they receive a small fee for each nutria they kill. Scientists are additionally attempting to manufacture an effective pesticide which kills the nutria in large numbers but which causes no harm to other animals or plants.

The third major problem is that people who use the river for recreation are damaging the plant while also creating water pollution. To reduce the harm caused by humans, conservationists are informing the public about the threatened status of the plant. This information includes warnings to be careful when near the plant, not to strike it with boats, not to swim near it, and not to dislodge it from its habitat. Boaters are also being advised to keep the river clean of pollution and are being fined when they dirty its waters.

A02

Directions You have 20 minutes to plan and write your response. Your response will be judged on the basis of the quality of your writing and on how well your response presents the points in the lecture and their relationship to the passage. Typically, an effective response will be 150-225 words.

Question Summarize the points made in the lecture, being sure to explain how they cast doubt on specific points made in the reading passage.

COPY CUT PASTE   Word Count : 0

A | Reading Passage

Read the following passage carefully. Try to understand what the main argument of the passage is.

One of the great maritime mysteries concerns the fate of the crew of the *Mary Celeste*. On December 4, 1872, the ship was located adrift near the Azores Islands in the Atlantic Ocean with the crew gone and a lifeboat missing. No sign of the crew has ever been found. Since then, people have speculated about what happened to make the crew abandon their seaworthy vessel. Numerous theories abound, but three are considered the most likely to be accurate.

There is a strong possibility that the weather caused the crew to depart the *Mary Celeste*. The ship's sails were tattered and found in awkward positions for sailing. In addition, water damage in many of the ship's cabins and deep water in the hold suggested that large waves had struck the ship. With the sails unusable, perhaps the crew deemed the ship unmanageable and therefore took to the lifeboat, which was subsequently lost at sea.

The *Mary Celeste* was transporting a large cargo of industrial alcohol, which was dangerous because its fumes could have leaked and built up in the cargo hold. If this had happened, the crew might have feared a massive explosion was about to occur. If something such as a small buildup of pressure blew the hatches off the cargo hold, the crew may have abandoned the ship to save their lives from a potentially catastrophic explosion.

A third theory centers on traces of blood found on the ship's deck as well as a sword. Some speculate that the crew mutinied, murdered the captain, and then departed on the lifeboat lest they be imprisoned and punished when the ship made port. Not wanting news of their misdeeds to be known, the survivors on the lifeboat would have kept quiet about their actions on board the *Mary Celeste*.

Vocabulary

- ☐ **fate** (n) an outcome; destiny
- ☐ **crew** (n) the people who work on a ship
- ☐ **adrift** (adj) floating without being controlled
- ☐ **abandon** (v) to give up and to depart
- ☐ **seaworthy** (adj) able to be sailed
- ☐ **tattered** (adj) being in pieces
- ☐ **fume** (n) a vapor; a gas
- ☐ **hatch** (n) an opening on a ship that passengers or cargo can pass through
- ☐ **hold** (n) a storage area on a ship
- ☐ **catastrophic** (adj) disastrous
- ☐ **mutiny** (v) to rebel against the captain of a ship
- ☐ **misdeed** (n) a crime; an illegal or improper action

◪ Outlining

Write an outline of the reading passage in the space provided.

Main Point

Argument ❶

Argument ❷

Argument ❸

◪ Paraphrasing Exercises

Read the following sentences. Then, paraphrase them. Be sure to include the key information in each sentence.

1   In addition, water damage in many of the ship's cabins and deep water in the hold suggested that large waves had struck the ship.

→

2   The *Mary Celeste* was transporting a large cargo of industrial alcohol, which was dangerous because its fumes could have leaked and built up in the cargo hold.

→

3   Not wanting news of their misdeeds to be known, the survivors on the lifeboat would have kept quiet about their actions on board the *Mary Celeste*.

→

Listening Lecture 🎧 A03

Listen to a lecture on the topic you just read about. Be sure to take notes while you listen.

◢ Note-Taking

Main Point _____

_____

Argument ❶ _____

_____

Argument ❷ _____

_____

Argument ❸ _____

_____

◢ Paraphrasing Exercises

Read the following sentences. Then, paraphrase them. Be sure to include the key information in each sentence.

1 Because the ship was in no danger of sinking, the captain surely wouldn't have ordered the crew to get into the small lifeboat.

→ _____

_____

2 Now the cargo, which was industrial alcohol, was known to leak fumes due to it being stored in wooden barrels back in the nineteenth century.

→ _____

_____

3 And while some people suspected the salvage crew might have killed everyone on the *Mary Celeste*, they were of high moral character and had never run afoul of the law before.

→ _____

_____

C | Combining the Main Points

Read the following sentences from the reading passage and listening lecture. Then, combine each pair of sentences by using the given patterns.

1 **Reading** There is a strong possibility that the weather caused the crew to depart the *Mary Celeste*. The ship's sails were tattered and found in awkward positions for sailing. In addition, water damage in many of the ship's cabins and deep water in the hold suggested that large waves had struck the ship.

Listening It's almost certainly true that the ship was damaged by the elements, but the weather did not make the ship unseaworthy. In fact, the salvage crew that found the *Mary Celeste* sailed her all the way to Gibraltar, a considerable distance.

→ **The professor acknowledges that** _____ **, yet**

he points out that _____ **.**

2 **Reading** If this had happened, the crew might have feared a massive explosion was about to occur. If something such as a small buildup of pressure blew the hatches off the cargo hold, the crew may have abandoned the ship to save their lives from a potentially catastrophic explosion.

Listening Yet when British experts in Gibraltar examined the ship, they found no sign of explosive damage or fire. All the cargo hatches were secure, and except for a few barrels that had leaked a bit, the cargo was secure.

→ **While the writer of the reading passage believes that** _____

_____ **, the**

professor states that _____

_____ **.**

3 **Reading** Some speculate that the crew mutinied, murdered the captain, and then departed on the lifeboat lest they be imprisoned and punished when the ship made port. Not wanting news of their misdeeds to be known, the survivors on the lifeboat would have kept quiet about their actions on board the *Mary Celeste*.

Listening In fact, what were believed to be human bloodstains found on the ship were later shown by experts not to be human blood at all. No crew members had a previous history of violent crime. And while some people suspected the salvage crew might have killed everyone on the *Mary Celeste*, they were of high moral character and had never run afoul of the law before.

→ **The professor remarks that** _____

_____ **. His declarations**

therefore challenge _____

_____ **.**

Completing the Essay

Complete the following essay which summarizes the points made in the lecture. Be sure to explain how they challenge specific claims made in the reading passage. Use the phrases to help you write your essay.

During his lecture, the professor discusses _____

_____

_____ .

The professor acknowledges that _____ , yet he points

out that _____ . He therefore shows that

_____

_____ .

Another theory is that _____

_____ . While the writer of the reading passage believes that

_____ ,

the professor states that _____

_____ .

Finally, the professor mentions _____ . The professor remarks

that _____

_____ . His declarations therefore challenge the one made in the reading passage

that _____ .

Ancient Greek historian Herodotus wrote about the Phoenicians in his work *The Histories*. He claimed that around 600 B.C., they circumnavigated Africa by sailing south from the Red Sea, west around the Cape of Good Hope, and then north alongside the western part of Africa, whereupon they entered the Mediterranean Sea through the Straits of Gibraltar. This journey took approximately three years to accomplish. Ever since Herodotus made his claim, others have been skeptical about it for a number of valid reasons.

To begin with, while the Phoenicians constructed good sailing ships, they were coast huggers not intended for rough, open seas. Their sails were square and therefore unable to do much more than catch a direct breeze, so the ships had little ability to tack into contrary winds. This would have been troublesome on the northward journey by Africa's west coast because the wind mostly blows from the north.

The Phoenicians also would have been venturing into the unknown since they would have been unfamiliar with the African coast, its currents, the locations of reefs, and the prevailing winds for nearly the entire journey. The chances are that their ships could not have survived those dangers and either attempted the journey but were forced to turn back or sank somewhere along the way.

Finally, the weather around the Cape of Good Hope is some of the worst in the world due to the strong winds and high waves. In other areas, the winds can be becalmed for weeks at a time. A recent attempt to recreate the voyage with a replica Phoenician ship proved the danger of the weather. The voyage only succeeded because the ship had satellite navigation aids, up-to-date weather reports, and an engine it used when the wind was not blowing.

A04

Directions You have 20 minutes to plan and write your response. Your response will be judged on the basis of the quality of your writing and on how well your response presents the points in the lecture and their relationship to the passage. Typically, an effective response will be 150-225 words.

Question Summarize the points made in the lecture, being sure to specifically explain how they answer the problems raised in the reading passage.

| COPY | CUT | PASTE | Word Count : 0 |

A | Reading Passage

Read the following passage carefully. Try to understand what the main argument of the passage is.

Large numbers of Americans spend countless hours each day commuting to and from work or school in major urban centers. To alleviate their transportation problems, some metropolises are proposing the constructing of high-speed express train systems to link suburbs and nearby cities to one another. These express trains would possess several advantages over cars, buses, and slower commuter trains. As a result, cities should put every effort into constructing high-speed express trains as quickly as possible.

One major benefit is that express trains can utilize existing railway systems whereas any increase in car and bus traffic would require new roads and extensive road maintenance to operate efficiently. Trains, however, can transport more people than cars and buses, so there would be fewer train trips required, and the wear and tear on railways would be much less than on roads since there would be less traffic. Thus cities could actually save money on construction and maintenance.

Express trains would reduce traffic congestion as well. While a single train can carry hundreds of passengers per journey, the same number of people must travel in hundreds of cars to reach their destinations, which can create massive traffic jams. Railways do not have to worry about traffic since their movements are tightly scheduled and controlled. Passengers always know when they will leave and arrive, but motorists cannot be sure of that.

A third benefit is that express trains can reduce pollution. A few trains carrying large numbers of passengers create less pollution than hundreds or thousands of vehicles on the roads. And when these cars idle on highways due to traffic jams, they produce even more pollution. Trains, on the other hand, expel much less pollution on a per-person basis.

Vocabulary

- ☐ **alleviate** *v* to ease; to make better or improve
- ☐ **metropolis** *n* a large city
- ☐ **link** *v* to connect; to join
- ☐ **extensive** *adj* widespread
- ☐ **wear and tear** *phr* deterioration
- ☐ **congestion** *n* crowding; blocking
- ☐ **massive** *adj* very large
- ☐ **motorist** *n* a person who drives a motor vehicle such as a car, truck, or bus
- ☐ **idle** *v* to remain motionless; to do nothing
- ☐ **expel** *v* to send out; to emit

◪ Outlining

Write an outline of the reading passage in the space provided.

Main Point _____

_____

Argument ❶ _____

_____

Argument ❷ _____

_____

Argument ❸ _____

_____

◪ Paraphrasing Exercises

Read the following sentences. Then, paraphrase them. Be sure to include the key information in each sentence.

1 Trains, however, can transport more people than cars and buses, so there would be fewer train trips required, and the wear and tear on railways would be much less than on roads since there would be less traffic.

→ _____

_____

2 While a single train can carry hundreds of passengers per journey, the same number of people must travel in hundreds of cars to reach their destinations, which can create massive traffic jams.

→ _____

_____

3 A few trains carrying large numbers of passengers create less pollution than hundreds or thousands of vehicles on the roads.

→ _____

_____

B | Listening Lecture 🎧 A05

Listen to a lecture on the topic you just read about. Be sure to take notes while you listen.

◢ Note-Taking

Main Point

Argument ❶

Argument ❷

Argument ❸

◢ Paraphrasing Exercises

Read the following sentences. Then, paraphrase them. Be sure to include the key information in each sentence.

1 Express trains in particular require high-grade rails and safe routes because they travel at faster speeds than regular trains.

→ _____

2 But in the southern and western parts of the country, cities and suburbs tend to be more spread out, so public transportation isn't practical.

→ _____

3 And when you consider that our existing rail systems don't allow trains to move quickly and suffer from plenty of delays, you'll realize that idling and slow-moving trains will expel even more pollution into the air.

→ _____

C | Combining the Main Points

Read the following sentences from the reading passage and listening lecture. Then, combine each pair of sentences by using the given patterns.

1 **Reading** Trains, however, can transport more people than cars and buses, so there would be fewer train trips required, and the wear and tear on railways would be much less than on roads since there would be less traffic. Thus cities could actually save money on construction and maintenance.

Listening Express trains in particular require high-grade rails and safe routes because they travel at faster speeds than regular trains. Just building a single high-speed rail system in one area can require billions of dollars.

→ The professor believes that _____ , which

is in opposition to the claim in the reading passage that _____

_____ .

2 **Reading** Express trains would reduce traffic congestion as well. While a single train can carry hundreds of passengers per journey, the same number of people must travel in hundreds of cars to reach their destinations, which can create massive traffic jams.

Listening But in the southern and western parts of the country, cities and suburbs tend to be more spread out, so public transportation isn't practical. People would have to drive their vehicles to stations, pay to park them, and then board trains. For those individuals, it would be easier and faster to drive.

→ The professor admits that _____ , but she

also points out that _____

_____ .

3 **Reading** A few trains carrying large numbers of passengers create less pollution than hundreds or thousands of vehicles on the roads.

Listening And when you consider that our existing rail systems don't allow trains to move quickly and suffer from plenty of delays, you'll realize that idling and slow-moving trains will expel even more pollution into the air.

→ Although the reading passage claims that _____

_____ , the professor disputes this notion. She says

_____ .

D | Completing the Essay

Complete the following essay which summarizes the points made in the lecture. Be sure to explain how they cast doubt on specific points made in the reading passage. Use the phrases to help you write your essay.

The professor covers _____ .

Her arguments against them _____

_____ .

Both the reading passage and the professor discuss _____ . The

professor mentions that _____ .

She believes that _____ , which is in opposition to

the claim in the reading passage that _____

_____ .

The professor's second argument concerns _____ . She admits that

_____ , but she also points out that

_____ .

Her argument thusly goes against the claim in the reading passage _____

_____ .

Last, although the reading passage claims that _____

_____ , the professor disputes this notion. She says _____

_____

_____ .

Zoning laws regulate the development of a region's land and are specifically focused on what structures can be built in various places. For the most part, zoning laws are designed to prevent incompatible structures, such as factories and schools, from being built alongside one another. Thus urban areas have many different zones. Among them are residential zones for housing and schools, business zones for offices, stores, and shopping malls, green zones for parks and recreation, and industrial zones for factories and other manufacturing centers. The zones provide benefits for their communities in a variety of ways.

One is that they preserve the property value of private land. For instance, homeowners prefer to live in regions which only have houses and schools and have small numbers of stores and office buildings. A person's home would lose much of its value if a large factory were suddenly erected across the street from it. The homeowner would consequently have trouble selling the house, which is something zoning laws prevent from happening.

Zoning laws further help maintain the integrity and safety of neighborhoods by preventing certain types of entertainment establishments from being built in residential zones. Most cities, as an example, do not permit nightclubs and bars to be opened near schools and housing areas. Zoning laws additionally preserve green lands in urban regions. Therefore, parks and recreation zones are safe from being developed for purposes that would destroy their natural beauty.

A third benefit of zoning laws is that they maintain the historical integrity of communities which are in danger of being developed for new, yet incompatible, purposes. In that way, they can enable neighborhoods with historical structures of significance to avoid being transformed into industrial or entertainment districts that can bring ruination to the older buildings.

A06

Directions You have 20 minutes to plan and write your response. Your response will be judged on the basis of the quality of your writing and on how well your response presents the points in the lecture and their relationship to the passage. Typically, an effective response will be 150-225 words.

Question Summarize the points made in the lecture, being sure to explain how they challenge specific arguments made in the reading passage.

COPY   CUT   PASTE   Word Count : 0

A | Reading Passage

Read the following passage carefully. Try to understand what the main argument of the passage is.

In the United States, invasive species, particularly fish and reptiles, are causing harm throughout the country. For example, the Burmese python is killing myriad birds and mammals in the Florida Everglades while Asian carp are causing problems in water habitats in the Great Lakes region. Many invasive species used to be household pets but were released into the wild and promptly reproduced rapidly since they have no natural predators. The government must introduce legislation to restrict the importing and selling of these animals to save the country's natural environment.

To begin with, pet shops selling exotic animals should be heavily regulated. Many store owners are careless and sell animals to anyone rather than only to those individuals who are able to provide quality care for exotic animals, which are much harder to raise than dogs or cats. The legislation should make it legal for animals to be seized and either returned to their countries of origin or terminated if the owners of stores are deemed to be selling them to irresponsible individuals.

The legislation should provide funding to examine the effects nonnative species pose to the environment, too. While it is obvious that the Burmese python is a source of trouble, it is not clear what other harm certain species are capable of causing. Once the studies are complete, if certain species are determined to be potentially harmful, they should be banned from the country.

Finally, there should be outright bans on the importation of various species of animals from foreign countries. Snakes and lizards in particular should not be permitted into the country. They can escape captivity easily and reproduce quickly. The best way to keep the United States safe should be to stop nonnative species of animals from entering the country in the first place.

Vocabulary

- **myriad** *adj* very many; a lot of
- **habitat** *n* an area where a certain plant or animal lives
- **legislation** *n* a law; a rule
- **restrict** *v* to put a limit on
- **terminate** *v* to kill
- **irresponsible** *adj* careless; lacking responsibility
- **potentially** *adv* possibly
- **outright** *adj* complete; absolute
- **captivity** *n* custody; imprisonment

◢ Outlining

Write an outline of the reading passage in the space provided.

Main Point _____

_____

Argument ❶ _____

_____

Argument ❷ _____

_____

Argument ❸ _____

_____

◢ Paraphrasing Exercises

Read the following sentences. Then, paraphrase them. Be sure to include the key information in each sentence.

1 Many store owners are careless and sell animals to anyone rather than only to those individuals who are able to provide quality care for exotic animals, which are much harder to raise than dogs or cats.

    → _____

    _____

2 Once the studies are complete, if certain species are determined to be potentially harmful, they should be banned from the country.

    → _____

    _____

3 The best way to keep the United States safe should be to stop nonnative species of animals from entering the country in the first place.

    → _____

    _____

Listening Lecture 🎧 A07

Listen to a lecture on the topic you just read about. Be sure to take notes while you listen.

◣ Note-Taking

Main Point _____

_____

Argument ❶ _____

_____

Argument ❷ _____

_____

Argument ❸ _____

_____

◣ Paraphrasing Exercises

Read the following sentences. Then, paraphrase them. Be sure to include the key information in each sentence.

1 First, the government simply doesn't have the manpower or capability to raid thousands of pet stores across the country, to seize the animals, and then to keep them caged up.

   → _____

   _____

2 Next, I don't see how scientists can study the effects nonnative species might have if they were released into the wild without, uh, well, actually releasing some animals into the wild to find out what will happen.

   → _____

   _____

3 If you ask me, it would actually be safer to permit the animals into the country legally so that we can know exactly where they are and who owns them.

   → _____

   _____

C | Combining the Main Points

Read the following sentences from the reading passage and listening lecture. Then, combine each pair of sentences by using the given patterns.

1 `Reading` The legislation should make it legal for animals to be seized and either returned to their countries of origin or terminated if the owners of stores are deemed to be selling them to irresponsible individuals.

`Listening` First, the government simply doesn't have the manpower or capability to raid thousands of pet stores across the country, to seize the animals, and then to keep them caged up. Second, the government would have to compensate the owners for their losses, and that could require millions, um, or even billions, of dollars in payments.

→ **First, the professor mentions that** _____

_____ **. Second, she points out that** _____

_____ **. In those ways, she goes against the argument in the reading passage**

that _____ .

2 `Reading` The legislation should provide funding to examine the effects nonnative species pose to the environment, too.

`Listening` Next, I don't see how scientists can study the effects nonnative species might have if they were released into the wild without actually releasing some animals into the wild to find out what will happen.

→ **Although the reading passage argues that** _____ **, the professor states that**

_____

_____ .

3 `Reading` Finally, there should be outright bans on the importation of various species of animals from foreign countries.

`Listening` If you ask me, it would actually be safer to permit the animals into the country legally so that we can know exactly where they are and who owns them.

→ **Unlike the reading passage, which argues in favor of** _____

_____ **, the professor thinks** _____

_____ .

D | Completing the Essay

Complete the following essay which summarizes the points made in the lecture. Be sure to explain how they cast doubt on specific points made in the reading passage. Use the phrases to help you write your essay.

While lecturing, the professor discusses _____
_____
_____ .

The professor doubts _____ .

First, she mentions that _____ . Second,

she points out that _____ . In those ways, she

goes against the argument in the reading passage that _____

_____ .

The professor also opposes _____ .

Although the reading passage argues that _____ , the professor states that _____

_____
_____ .

The final point the professor makes _____ . She claims that

_____ . So unlike

the reading passage, which argues in favor of _____ ,

she thinks _____ .

Around the world, certain animals have seen their habitats reduced in size to the point that they have disappeared entirely from some lands. For instance, lions and elephants once roamed throughout North America, wolves and beavers used to thrive in Britain, and Siberian tigers lived all over Northeast Asia in the past. Today, some conservationists are attempting to reintroduce some species of animals to the lands they lived on before. There are many benefits to doing so, and these efforts should be encouraged.

The primary reason species are reintroduced is to restore a region to its natural state of equilibrium. In many cases, the species which went extinct in an area had acted as a check on other animals. For instance, the wolf once controlled the deer population in the Yellowstone National Park region in the United States. However, when the wolf disappeared, the deer population exploded, causing great harm to the ecosystem due to all the foliage it consumed. Once the wolf was reintroduced to Yellowstone in the 1990s, the deer overpopulation problem was swiftly solved.

Some animals are reintroduced to regions simply to atone for wrongs caused by human activities. In that way, nature is allowed to resume its course, which had gone astray because of humans. This is the reasoning for the plan to reintroduce the beaver to Britain. Hunting and human encroachment on its land caused it to disappear from the country. However, if all goes well, there will soon be beavers living in Britain again.

Lastly, some people promote reintroducing animals to environments to prove the viability of breeding animals in captivity. First, individuals raise animals on farms or ranches and then release them into the wild. This method has allowed for the successful reintroduction of numerous species into their former habitats.

🎧 A08

Directions You have 20 minutes to plan and write your response. Your response will be judged on the basis of the quality of your writing and on how well your response presents the points in the lecture and their relationship to the passage. Typically, an effective response will be 150-225 words.

Question Summarize the points made in the lecture, being sure to explain how they challenge specific claims made in the reading passage.

COPY   CUT   PASTE   Word Count : 0

A Reading Passage

Read the following passage carefully. Try to understand what the main argument of the passage is.

Ceramic objects such as pottery are major sources of information about the past for archaeologists. Thanks to their durability, which enables the ceramics to last for thousands of years, they are commonly found at dig sites. While the purposes of most ceramic objects are obvious, there are times when the reason that an item was made eludes archaeologists. Ceramic disks are one such example. The purposes of these relatively flat, circular pieces of pottery are unknown, yet archaeologists have a few seemingly valid theories regarding how they were utilized.

Some experts theorize that the ceramic disks were once used for cooking. On account of their flat surfaces and ability to withstand high heat, the disks might have been used as frying pans in ancient times. Perhaps they were placed on tripods or balanced on rocks over open fires, and then people cooked meat, fish, or other foods atop them.

A second possibility is that they were created to be musical instruments. Large disks could have been used as drums. These disks would have been held in one hand or balanced on a wooden stand or frame while the musician then beat on the surface of the disk with a heavy stick in order to produce a sound. Disks of various sizes would have been able to create different tones.

Other archaeologists hypothesize that the disks were utilized as mirrors. If they were highly polished, people could have used them for their reflective surfaces. These would have been popular in societies that had discovered neither metallurgy nor how to make glassware. While the images they created would not have been outstanding, they still would have enabled people to view themselves.

Vocabulary

- **archaeologist** _n_ a person who studies cultures and civilizations from the past
- **durability** _n_ the toughness of something
- **elude** _v_ to escape; to avoid
- **seemingly** _adv_ apparently
- **valid** _adj_ legitimate; accurate
- **theorize** _v_ to believe; to create a theory about something
- **withstand** _v_ to resist
- **tripod** _n_ a stand or support that has three legs
- **hypothesize** _v_ to come up with an idea about something
- **metallurgy** _n_ the art of working with and shaping metal
- **glassware** _n_ items that are made of glass

▌ Outlining

Write an outline of the reading passage in the space provided.

Main Point _____

_____

Argument ❶ _____

_____

Argument ❷ _____

_____

Argument ❸ _____

_____

▌ Paraphrasing Exercises

Read the following sentences. Then, paraphrase them. Be sure to include the key information in each sentence.

1 On account of their flat surfaces and ability to withstand high heat, the disks might have been used as frying pans in ancient times.

→ _____

_____

2 These disks would have been held in one hand or balanced on a wooden stand or frame while the musician then beat on the surface of the disk with a heavy stick in order to produce a sound.

→ _____

_____

3 While the images they created would not have been outstanding, they still would have enabled people to view themselves.

→ _____

_____

B | Listening Lecture A09

Listen to a lecture on the topic you just read about. Be sure to take notes while you listen.

Note-Taking

Main Point ______________________________

____

Argument ❶ ______________________________

____

Argument ❷ ______________________________

____

Argument ❸ ______________________________

____

Paraphrasing Exercises

Read the following sentences. Then, paraphrase them. Be sure to include the key information in each sentence.

1 And no disks found have any of those marks on them, so since there's no physical evidence, I think we can discount this theory.

→ ______________________________

____

2 Ceramics are a poor means of transmitting musical tones, which is in evidence today by the lack of musical instruments made of ceramics.

→ ______________________________

____

3 A third prominent theory—that ceramic disks were once mirrors—is laughable for the simple reason that ceramics don't have highly reflective surfaces.

→ ______________________________

____

C | Combining the Main Points

Read the following sentences from the reading passage and listening lecture. Then, combine each pair of sentences by using the given patterns.

1 **Reading** On account of their flat surfaces and ability to withstand high heat, the disks might have been used as frying pans in ancient times.

Listening Do you see any scorch marks, discoloration from fire, or food residue on it . . . ? I don't. And no disks found have any of those marks on them, so since there's no physical evidence, I think we can discount this theory.

→ The professor points out _____ , so

this disproves the notion in the reading passage that _____

_____ .

2 **Reading** A second possibility is that they were created to be musical instruments. Large disks could have been used as drums.

Listening Ceramics are a poor means of transmitting musical tones, which is in evidence today by the lack of musical instruments made of ceramics. Hollowed-out wood or cured animal hides stretched over wooden frames were the preferred means of making drums in ancient times, not ceramics.

→ In stating that _____

_____ , the professor

proves that the idea that _____ .

3 **Reading** Other archaeologists hypothesize that the disks were utilized as mirrors. If they were highly polished, people could have used them for their reflective surfaces.

Listening A third prominent theory—that ceramic disks were once mirrors—is laughable for the simple reason that ceramics don't have highly reflective surfaces. Sure, they can reflect images, but not well enough to serve as mirrors.

→ While both the professor and the reading passage admit that _____ ,

the professor says that _____ .

D | Completing the Essay

Complete the following essay which summarizes the points made in the lecture. Be sure to explain how they cast doubt on specific points made in the reading passage. Use the phrases to help you write your essay.

The professor talks to the students about _____

_____. In the process of his lecture, the professor discusses _____

_____.

The first theory mentioned is that _____. The professor, however,

_____. He points out _____, so this

disproves the notion in the reading passage that _____

_____.

The second theory claims that _____. The professor doubts _____

_____. In stating _____

_____, the professor proves that the idea that _____

_____.

The third theory is _____. But the professor _____.

While both the professor and the reading passage admit that _____, the professor

says that _____

_____.

Located in Giza, Egypt, alongside the great pyramids, the Sphinx is a massive monolith depicting a mythical creature possessing the body of a lion and the head of a human. According to many experts, the Sphinx was built around 2550 B.C. during the reign of Pharaoh Khafre. However, this date is disputed by a large number of Egyptologists, many of whom believe it was built hundreds—or even thousands—of years prior to Khafre's rule.

One reason experts believe the Sphinx is more than 4,500 years old concerns the weathering of the statue. It was long believed that windblown sand was the cause of the eroding of the Sphinx, yet a new theory maintains that the Sphinx's weathering pattern was caused by falling water instead. The Sphinx has vertical erosion patterns, which indicate rain, whereas horizontal erosion patterns, which are lacking, would be proof of erosion by wind and sand. Since Khafre's time, Egypt has not experienced enough rainfall to cause a significant amount of water erosion. However, it is known that centuries prior to Khafre's reign, Egypt got much greater amounts of rain. This was likely when the Sphinx became weathered.

Another problem is that there are no inscriptions in hieroglyphics anywhere indicating Khafre built it. The Egyptians often left written records about who had commissioned certain buildings, and Khafre certainly would have taken credit for the Sphinx had he been responsible for making it. Thus the absence of written proof shows that the Sphinx likely existed long before Khafre lived.

Finally, many Egyptologists don't believe that the original face of the Sphinx was that of Khafre. The Sphinx's head shows evidence of having been worked on numerous times. In all likelihood, the Sphinx existed when Khafre became the pharaoh, but he had its face redone to resemble his own.

🎧 A10

Directions You have 20 minutes to plan and write your response. Your response will be judged on the basis of the quality of your writing and on how well your response presents the points in the lecture and their relationship to the passage. Typically, an effective response will be 150-225 words.

Question Summarize the points made in the lecture, being sure to explain how they challenge specific claims made in the reading passage.

COPY   CUT   PASTE   Word Count : 0

A | Reading Passage

Read the following passage carefully. Try to understand what the main argument of the passage is.

Every company strives to be as prosperous as possible and to maximize its profits. However, most businesses eventually reach a plateau, whereupon their ability to improve upon their success becomes elusive. When this happens to companies, there are several ways they can adjust in order to continue growing and to make themselves more successful.

One method large numbers of firms rely upon is to tweak their existing products to create similar, but new, items. For example, companies that produce household cleaning products may affix labels to them announcing their "new and improved" formulas. They are essentially selling the same products but with slightly different contents. Convinced that the products they like have been made even better, existing customers often buy more of these items while new customers may be induced to start buying them as well.

Selling ancillary products connected to a main product is another method frequently guaranteed to increase sales and profits. The automobile industry has been doing this for years. While they make the bulk of their money from car sales, by selling accessories for vehicles, companies can further increase their revenues. Computer companies act in a similar manner as they sell various add-ons that can make computers more powerful or provide them with greater functionality.

Some companies simply branch out from their core products and start selling other completely unrelated ones. While this is a challenging venture, successful companies can elevate their sales to much higher levels. Sony, a Japanese company, has followed this method to perfection. It began as a transistor radio producer but, over time, shifted to producing other electronic products such as televisions and video game consoles. Later, it entered the music and moviemaking businesses. Its innovating has helped make it one of the world's most successful companies.

Vocabulary

- **plateau** *n* a period of little or no growth
- **elusive** *adj* hard to find
- **tweak** *v* to make small changes to
- **affix** *v* to attach
- **induce** *v* to convince a person to do something
- **ancillary** *adj* auxiliary
- **functionality** *n* usage; utility
- **branch out** *phr* to expand
- **innovate** *v* to create, do, or think of something new

◢ Outlining

Write an outline of the reading passage in the space provided.

Main Point

Argument ❶

Argument ❷

Argument ❸

◢ Paraphrasing Exercises

Read the following sentences. Then, paraphrase them. Be sure to include the key information in each sentence.

1   Convinced that the products they like have been made even better, existing customers often buy more of these items while new customers may be induced to start buying them as well.

    →

2   Computer companies act in a similar manner as they sell various add-ons that can make computers more powerful or provide them with greater functionality.

    →

3   Some companies simply branch out from their core products and start selling other completely unrelated ones.

    →

B Listening Lecture 🎧 A11

Listen to a lecture on the topic you just read about. Be sure to take notes while you listen.

◤ Note-Taking

Main Point _____

_____

Argument ❶ _____

_____

Argument ❷ _____

_____

Argument ❸ _____

_____

◤ Paraphrasing Exercises

Read the following sentences. Then, paraphrase them. Be sure to include the key information in each sentence.

1   It didn't take long for the company to recognize the mistake it had made and to start selling Coke with the original recipe again.

   → _____

   _____

2   By the time I left, I was so mad that I had decided never to return to that store again.

   → _____

   _____

3   The companies have to spend vast fortunes on research and development, production, and marketing, but people don't associate them with the new products, so customers don't purchase them.

   → _____

   _____

C Combining the Main Points

Read the following sentences from the reading passage and listening lecture. Then, combine each pair of sentences by using the given patterns.

1 **Reading**   One method large numbers of firms rely upon is to tweak their existing products to create similar, but new, items. For example, companies that produce household cleaning products may affix labels to them announcing their "new and improved" formulas.

   Listening   I remember back in the 1980s when Coca-Cola changed the formula for Coke. New Coke was an absolute failure. People hated the way it tasted, and sales dropped dramatically. It didn't take long for the company to recognize the mistake it had made and to start selling Coke with the original recipe again.

→ **By noting that** _____

   _____ **, the professor casts doubt on the notion in the reading passage that** _____

   _____ .

2 **Reading**   Selling ancillary products connected to a main product is another method frequently guaranteed to increase sales and profits.

   Listening   All I wanted was a phone, but the salesperson kept trying to convince me to buy accessories, such as a recharger and a case, for it. By the time I left, I was so mad that I had decided never to return to that store.

→ **The author of the reading passage claims that** _____

   _____ **, but the professor argues that** _____

   _____ .

3 **Reading**   Some companies simply branch out from their core products and start selling other completely unrelated ones. While this is a challenging venture, successful companies can elevate their sales to much higher levels. Sony, a Japanese company, has followed this method to perfection.

   Listening   Well, the companies have to spend vast fortunes on research and development, production, and marketing, but people don't associate them with the new products, so customers don't purchase them. To be honest, entering a new market is a great way for a company to bankrupt itself.

→ **The author of the reading passage cites** _____

   However, the professor points out that _____

   _____ .

D | Completing the Essay

Complete the following essay which summarizes the points made in the lecture. Be sure to explain how they cast doubt on specific points made in the reading passage. Use the phrases to help you write your essay.

Both the lecture and the reading passage focus _____.

While the author of the reading passage _____

_____ , the professor explains _____ .

The professor first examines _____

_____ . By noting that

_____ , he casts doubt

on the notion in the reading passage that _____.

The professor also discusses _____

_____ . The author of the reading passage claims that _____

_____ , but the professor argues that _____

_____ .

Finally, both the professor and the reading passage mention that _____

_____ . The author of the reading passage cites _____

_____ . However, the professor points out that _____

_____ .

When companies have goods and services to sell, they often use advertising to let customers know about them. The basic principle behind advertising is to get a message to as many people as possible for the lowest price. Traditionally, companies used printed ads in newspapers and magazines. In recent years though, online advertising has emerged as a better way to inform customers about products.

One advantage of online ads is that they can reach far more people than printed ads. After all, newspapers and magazines have limited print runs—often in the hundreds or thousands—but literally anyone around the world with an Internet connection can see an online advertisement by clicking on a certain website. Since far more people can view online ads, companies are increasingly budgeting more money for them rather than for printed ones.

In addition, online ads tend to be cheaper than printed ads. The prices of most online ads are determined by the number of people clicking on them. Since businesses can limit the number of clicks per month, they can guarantee the sizes of their ad budgets. On the other hand, businesses pay flat fees, which can be extremely expensive, for printed ads. A full-page color advertisement in *USA Today*, an American newspaper, costs more than $200,000. Ads in other exclusive newspapers or magazines can cost tens of thousands of dollars as well.

A third benefit is that online ads are better suited than printed ads for specialized markets. For instance, a company selling sporting equipment would be much better off advertising on websites that provide sports news than it would in a local newspaper. After all, the readers of sports news are more likely to purchase sporting equipment than random readers of a local newspaper, who probably have other interests.

🎧 A12

Directions You have 20 minutes to plan and write your response. Your response will be judged on the basis of the quality of your writing and on how well your response presents the points in the lecture and their relationship to the passage. Typically, an effective response will be 150-225 words.

Question Summarize the points made in the lecture, being sure to explain how they challenge specific arguments made in the reading passage.

COPY   CUT   PASTE   Word Count : 0

A | Reading Passage

Read the following passage carefully. Try to understand what the main argument of the passage is.

Chesapeake Bay is one of the great aquatic ecosystems in the eastern part of the United States. In recent decades, it has developed an increasingly unhealthy environment, but efforts to improve the bay and the surrounding area are currently underway.

For decades, overfishing was a huge problem in the bay. This was particularly true of the blue crab, one of the region's major marine creatures. In the past, fishermen indiscriminately caught blue crabs and frequently pulled up spawning females. One year, an estimated 60% of all female blue crabs were caught, which caused the crabs' numbers to plummet. However, quotas limiting the number of crabs, especially females, which can be caught have been implemented, so the blue crab population is beginning to recover in Chesapeake Bay.

There is a great deal of farmland around Chesapeake Bay. Unfortunately, farmers inadvertently polluted the water because of the chemical fertilizers they used for years. When it rained, the nitrogen and phosphorous in the fertilizer combined with rainwater and found their way into the bay. This created unhealthy algae blooms, which absorbed large amounts of oxygen in the water and killed fish. Since 2009, strict controls have been placed on chemical usage and runoff, consequently reducing the amount of pollutants entering the bay.

The bay itself has become increasingly polluted, so people are contemplating ways to increase its oyster population. Oysters are filter feeders which pass water through their bodies to extract food particles in it. In the process, they also remove pollutants from the water. A species of Asian oysters is particularly adept at that since it is larger, faster growing, and more disease resistant than local oysters. Plans to introduce these oysters to the bay in the hope that they can help clean it up are presently being developed.

Vocabulary

- ☐ **ecosystem** *n* all of the organic and inorganic elements that interact in a certain area
- ☐ **indiscriminately** *adv* broadly; without concern
- ☐ **quota** *n* a set number of something that is permitted
- ☐ **inadvertently** *adv* accidentally
- ☐ **algae bloom** *phr* a large mass of tiny organisms on a body of water
- ☐ **pollutant** *n* something that causes an area to become unclear
- ☐ **contemplate** *v* to think about; to consider
- ☐ **adept** *adj* skilled
- ☐ **disease resistant** *phr* able to avoid getting certain sicknesses or illnesses
- ☐ **eradicate** *v* to kill; to eliminate

■ Outlining

Write an outline of the reading passage in the space provided.

Main Point

Argument ❶

Argument ❷

Argument ❸

■ Paraphrasing Exercises

Read the following sentences. Then, paraphrase them. Be sure to include the key information in each sentence.

1 However, quotas limiting the number of crabs, especially females, which can be caught have been implemented, so the blue crab population is beginning to recover in Chesapeake Bay.

→

2 Since 2009, strict controls have been placed on chemical usage and runoff, consequently reducing the amount of pollutants entering the bay.

→

3 A species of Asian oysters is particularly adept at that since it is larger, faster growing, and more disease resistant than local oysters.

→

Listening Lecture 🎧 A13

Listen to a lecture on the topic you just read about. Be sure to take notes while you listen.

◢ Note-Taking

Main Point _____

_____

Argument ❶ _____

_____

Argument ❷ _____

_____

Argument ❸ _____

_____

◢ Paraphrasing Exercises

Read the following sentences. Then, paraphrase them. Be sure to include the key information in each sentence.

1   Remember that there are numerous small communities whose residents depend on fishing for their livelihoods, so quotas will reduce their ability to make a living.

    → _____

    _____

2   Combined, they cause a significant amount of harm to the bay, but politicians are ignoring these issues, so they will continue to be problems in the future.

    → _____

    _____

3   They could additionally cause all sorts of problems, especially if they migrate to other regions along the eastern seaboard.

    → _____

    _____

C | Combining the Main Points

Read the following sentences from the reading passage and listening lecture. Then, combine each pair of sentences by using the given patterns.

1 **Reading** However, quotas limiting the number of crabs, especially females, which can be caught have been implemented, so the blue crab population is beginning to recover in Chesapeake Bay.

Listening For one thing, establishing quotas on the number of fish that can be caught will definitely help fish stocks increase, yet it will simultaneously hurt local fishermen. Remember that there are numerous small communities whose residents depend on fishing for their livelihoods, so quotas will reduce their ability to make a living.

→ **Although the professor agrees with the reading passage that** _____

_____ **, she points out a negative aspect of the quotas. They are**

_____ .

2 **Reading** Since 2009, strict controls have been placed on chemical usage and runoff, consequently reducing the amount of pollutants entering the bay.

Listening Well, sewage from towns and cities and runoff from forests sprayed with insecticides both wind up in the bay. Combined, they cause a significant amount of harm to the bay, but politicians are ignoring these issues, so they will continue to be problems in the future.

→ **The professor states that** _____ ,

so unlike the author of the reading passage, _____ .

3 **Reading** A species of Asian oysters is particularly adept at that since it is larger, faster growing, and more disease resistant than local oysters. Plans to introduce these oysters to the bay in the hope that they can help clean it up are presently being developed.

Listening Asian oysters are a nonnative species that would likely grow out of control and replace the native oysters. They could additionally cause all sorts of problems, especially if they migrate to other regions along the eastern seaboard. We simply shouldn't be introducing invasive species into the bay.

→ **The author of the reading passage supports** _____ **, but the professor speaks strongly**

against it. She believes that _____ .

D | Completing the Essay

Complete the following essay which summarizes the points made in the lecture. Be sure to explain how they cast doubt on specific points made in the reading passage. Use the phrases to help you write your essay.

The professor's lecture provides a pessimistic view of _____

_____ . She has a much different opinion than the author of the reading passage, who is

_____ .

To begin with, the professor comments on _____ .

Although the professor agrees with the reading passage that _____

_____ , she points out a negative aspect of the quotas. They are _____

_____ .

A second point the professor discusses is _____ . Like the author of the reading passage, she

approves _____ . Yet she states that

_____ , so unlike the author of the

reading passage, she thinks _____ .

The third point mentioned is _____

_____ . The author of the reading passage supports _____ , but the professor speaks strongly

against it. She believes that _____ .

The lionfish is a tropical species native to the Indian and Pacific oceans. Noted for its vibrant colors, the lionfish was once a prized aquarium fish, especially in North America. However, its voracious appetite led to it attacking other fish kept in the same aquariums and resulted in many owners disposing of their lionfish in nearby waterways. While many lionfish died in the wild, they have found homes in the Caribbean Sea and the Western Atlantic Ocean, where their numbers are exploding. They are consuming large numbers of fish in coral reefs and being general nuisances, so people are devising ways to get rid of them.

Few fish actively hunt the lionfish, but the grouper is one. Yet the grouper is a popular food fish around the world, so fishermen commonly catch it. Some people have proposed enacting quotas on the number of groupers caught in areas with numerous lionfish. By doing so, the grouper population can increase, and then there will be more groupers to hunt lionfish.

Fishermen are now being encouraged not to release any lionfish they catch but to kill them even if they have no plans to eat them. Divers with spear guns are similarly being asked to shoot any lionfish they find, especially those living in coral reefs. While the fishermen and divers may not kill large numbers of lionfish, they can actively reduce their numbers.

People living in tropical areas are promoting the consumption of lionfish. The fish, which taste delicious, are considered a delicacy in China. By educating people in the United States and other countries about how good lionfish tastes, demand for the fish should increase, so more fishermen will start catching them. This should result in there being fewer lionfish in some regions.

🎧 A14

Directions You have 20 minutes to plan and write your response. Your response will be judged on the basis of the quality of your writing and on how well your response presents the points in the lecture and their relationship to the passage. Typically, an effective response will be 150-225 words.

Question Summarize the points made in the lecture, being sure to explain how they challenge specific arguments made in the reading passage.

COPY   CUT   PASTE   **Word Count : 0**

A Reading Passage

Read the following passage carefully. Try to understand what the main argument of the passage is.

One unusual type of behavior that some birds engage in is known as anting. This may involve a bird picking up individual ants in its beak and rubbing them all over its feathers, or a bird may lie down in an ant nest and allow the insects to crawl on its entire body. Ornithologists have long been confused by this behavior, yet they have managed to come up with a few hypotheses regarding why birds do anting.

The prevailing theory is that birds use anting as a part of their molting ritual. When birds molt, they lose their old feathers so that new ones can grow in their place. This theory is popular since ornithologists have observed that anting usually occurs in late summer or early fall, which is also when molting takes place. They believe birds use ant secretions to soothe their skin after it becomes irritated when they are molting.

Another notion is that birds use ant secretions to remove parasites such as lice and mites from their bodies. Ants sometimes secrete formic acid, which laboratory tests have confirmed can kill lice and mites on birds. Thus ornithologists believe that birds essentially take baths in formic acid secretions to remove unwanted parasites, thereby making their bodies cleaner.

A third idea is that anting is a way for birds to prepare ants to be eaten. When birds come into physical contact with ants, the insects' natural defenses cause them to start secreting defensive liquids. While these liquids do not harm the birds' feathers and skin, they could be harmful if they are ingested. So birds essentially cause the ants to deplete these secretions in order to make them edible. Once the anting process is done, birds can safely consume the ants.

Vocabulary

☐ **ornithologist** *n* a scientist who studies birds

☐ **prevailing** *adj* dominant; main; primary

☐ **molt** *v* to lose one's feathers so that new ones may grow in their place

☐ **soothe** *v* to ease

☐ **irritated** *adj* bothered; itchy

☐ **parasite** *n* an organism that harms the host that it lives on

☐ **mite** *n* a tiny parasite

☐ **secrete** *v* to release a substance from one's body

☐ **confirm** *v* to learn that something is true or correct

☐ **ingest** *v* to take something into one's body, such as by eating it

☐ **deplete** *v* to use up entirely or almost entirely

▮ Outlining

Write an outline of the reading passage in the space provided.

Main Point _____

_____

Argument ❶ _____

_____

Argument ❷ _____

_____

Argument ❸ _____

_____

▮ Paraphrasing Exercises

Read the following sentences. Then, paraphrase them. Be sure to include the key information in each sentence.

1 This theory is popular since ornithologists have observed that anting usually occurs in late summer or early fall, which is also when molting takes place.

→ _____

_____

2 Thus ornithologists believe that birds essentially take baths in formic acid secretions to remove unwanted parasites, thereby making their bodies cleaner.

→ _____

_____

3 When birds come into physical contact with ants, the insects' natural defenses cause them to start secreting defensive liquids.

→ _____

_____

B | Listening Lecture 🎧 A15

Listen to a lecture on the topic you just read about. Be sure to take notes while you listen.

◤ Note-Taking

Main Point _____

_____

Argument ❶ _____

_____

Argument ❷ _____

_____

Argument ❸ _____

_____

◤ Paraphrasing Exercises

Read the following sentences. Then, paraphrase them. Be sure to include the key information in each sentence.

1 We don't really know if birds get irritated skin from molting and if the acidic liquids produced by the ants help relieve any itching sensations.

→ _____

_____

2 It's true that formic acid can kill many parasites, but attempts at getting birds to engage in anting in laboratories have failed to reach any conclusions.

→ _____

_____

3 In addition, birds have been observed rubbing millipedes, beetles, and even flowers on their feathers, but the birds weren't seen eating those things afterward.

→ _____

_____

C | Combining the Main Points

Read the following sentences from the reading passage and listening lecture. Then, combine each pair of sentences by using the given patterns.

1 **Reading** They believe birds use ant secretions to soothe their skin after it becomes irritated when they are molting.

Listening We don't really know if birds get irritated skin from molting and if the acidic liquids produced by the ants help relieve any itching sensations. It could be a complete coincidence that birds do both activities around the same time.

→ The author of the reading passage _____ , but the professor says _____

_____ .

2 **Reading** Another notion is that birds use ant secretions to remove parasites such as lice and mites from their bodies. Ants sometimes secrete formic acid, which laboratory tests have confirmed can kill lice and mites on birds.

Listening It's true that formic acid can kill many parasites, but attempts at getting birds to engage in anting in laboratories have failed to reach any conclusions. In addition, you should be aware that nearly all birds have parasites on their skin and feathers, but not all birds engage in anting. Only some species do.

→ The professor admits that _____ , but he comments that _____

_____ .

3 **Reading** When birds come into physical contact with ants, the insects' natural defenses cause them to start secreting defensive liquids. While these liquids do not harm the birds' feathers and skin, they could be harmful if they are ingested.

Listening That was in a controlled environment, so the results are inconclusive. In addition, birds have been observed rubbing millipedes, beetles, and even flowers on their feathers, but the birds weren't seen eating those things afterward.

→ According to the reading passage, _____ . While the

professor acknowledges that this _____ , he also remarks that

_____ .

D | Completing the Essay

Complete the following essay which summarizes the points made in the lecture. Be sure to explain how they cast doubt on specific points made in the reading passage. Use the phrases to help you write your essay.

The professor's lecture is about _____

_____. The author of the reading passage_____ , but

the professor _____ .

The first theory the professor mentions is that _____

_____ . The author of the reading passage _____ , but

the professor says _____ .

Another hypothesis proposed in the reading passage is that _____

_____ . The professor admits that _____ , but he

comments that _____

_____ .

A final theory the professor disregards is that _____

_____ . According to the reading passage, _____ .

While the professor acknowledges that _____ , he also remarks that

_____ .

The mountain yellow-legged frog was once common in the Sierra Nevada Mountains in Southern California, yet its numbers are in such steep decline today that it has been placed on the endangered species list. The reason for its decline has been attributed to three different factors, all of which have combined to devastate the mountain yellow-legged frog population.

The first problem has to do with the introduction of trout into the lakes and streams in the Sierra Nevada Mountains in the late nineteenth century, which disturbed the balance in the ecosystem there. Trout were a nonnative species in that region, and they quickly grew in numbers, primarily by feeding on mountain yellow-legged frog tadpoles and juveniles. Prior to the introduction of the trout, the frogs had no aquatic predators, so it was not instinctive for them to flee from the trout.

A second problem involves the various pesticides that have been utilized to kill pests both on trees and farmland for many years. During periods of rain or snow, the pesticides combine with the water and enter the local water system. They have therefore contaminated the water and wound up killing large numbers of frogs. Examinations of dead frogs have shown that many of them contained excessive amounts of pesticides in their bodies when they died.

A third problem that has affected the environment in which the frog lives is the growth of a deadly fungus in the region. This fungus attacks adult frogs and destroys the keratin in their bodies. Keratin comprises a signification portion of the skeletons and teeth of frogs, so their entire bodies become weakened and result in the frogs dying. Some frogs die as quickly as two weeks after becoming infected with the fungus.

🎧 A16

Directions You have 20 minutes to plan and write your response. Your response will be judged on the basis of the quality of your writing and on how well your response presents the points in the lecture and their relationship to the passage. Typically, an effective response will be 150-225 words.

Question Summarize the points made in the lecture, being sure to explain how they challenge specific claims made in the reading passage.

| COPY | CUT | PASTE | Word Count : 0 |

A | Reading Passage

Read the following passage carefully. Try to understand what the main argument of the passage is.

Cheatgrass is an invasive plant found in North America which is threatening to outcompete native grasses and other plants. It grows rapidly and can reproduce faster than most native grasses, so it can take better advantage of the natural resources in the areas it grows. It is also able to spread rapidly since its seeds are blown by the wind and carried by water and animals. As a result, the plant has become a nuisance that many people wish to eradicate.

One method that has met with success has been for people physically to destroy cheatgrass by cutting it with mowers, tilling it under the ground, or pulling it up by its roots. This is a labor-intensive method so is usually only done for small infestations rather than large-scale ones. In addition, fires are effective at killing cheatgrass, so people often use them in conjunction with other methods to rid themselves of it.

A more effective method that farmers have discovered is to allow their livestock to graze on land in which cheatgrass is growing. When cheatgrass first starts sprouting in spring, it contains high levels of protein and is therefore beneficial when consumed by livestock, particularly cattle. The best time for animals to graze on cheatgrass is the first six to eight weeks after it emerges from the ground.

It is also possible to remove cheatgrass through chemical means. Herbicides can be sprayed from backpack containers by individuals covering small areas, or they may be sprayed from motorized equipment or by crop dusters if there are particularly large infestations. The most effective time to utilize herbicides is in fall before the first frost as the plants become dormant during winter when it becomes too cold. In spring, herbicides are also effective right when the plants start growing.

Vocabulary

☐ **outcompete** (v) to do better than someone or something else at the same thing

☐ **nuisance** (n) an annoyance; a bother

☐ **eradicate** (v) to kill; to eliminate

☐ **till** (v) to dig up the ground, often in preparation for farming

☐ **labor-intensive** (adj) requiring a lot of work

☐ **in conjunction with** (phr) together with

☐ **sprout** (v) to come up from the ground

☐ **livestock** (n) animals such as cows, pigs, and chickens that are raised on farms

☐ **crop duster** (n) a small plane that spreads chemicals on fields

☐ **dormant** (adj) inactive

◢ Outlining

Write an outline of the reading passage in the space provided.

Main Point

_____

_____

Argument ❶

_____

_____

Argument ❷

_____

_____

Argument ❸

_____

_____

◢ Paraphrasing Exercises

Read the following sentences. Then, paraphrase them. Be sure to include the key information in each sentence.

1 One method that has met with success has been for people physically to destroy cheatgrass by cutting it with mowers, tilling it under the ground, or pulling it up by its roots.

→ _____

_____

2 When cheatgrass first starts sprouting in spring, it contains high levels of protein and is therefore beneficial when consumed by livestock, particularly cattle.

→ _____

_____

3 Herbicides can be sprayed from backpack containers by individuals covering small areas, or they may be sprayed from motorized equipment or by crop dusters if there are particularly large infestations.

→ _____

_____

B | Listening Lecture 🎧 A17

Listen to a lecture on the topic you just read about. Be sure to take notes while you listen.

◢ Note-Taking

Main Point _____

_____

Argument ❶ _____

_____

Argument ❷ _____

_____

Argument ❸ _____

_____

◢ Paraphrasing Exercises

Read the following sentences. Then, paraphrase them. Be sure to include the key information in each sentence.

1 Only experts should try to burn cheatgrass lest the people doing it wind up unintentionally burning large areas of land.

→ _____

_____

2 Livestock aren't allowed on most public lands, so farmers can remove the cheatgrass growing on their land, but they can't do anything about the public lands adjoining their property.

→ _____

_____

3 They're also expensive, and they harm the grasses and other plants growing alongside cheatgrass.

→ _____

_____

C Combining the Main Points

Read the following sentences from the reading passage and listening lecture. Then, combine each pair of sentences by using the given patterns.

1 **Reading** One method that has met with success has been for people physically to destroy cheatgrass by cutting it with mowers, tilling it under the ground, or pulling it up by its roots.

Listening In addition, those two methods don't kill the plant since it grows back. Thus people have to keep mowing or tilling it, which requires a great deal of work. So does pulling it out of the ground.

→ For example, the first proposal is to _____

_____ . The professor finds fault with these solutions though.

She declares that _____

_____ .

2 **Reading** A more effective method that farmers have discovered is to allow their livestock to graze on land in which cheatgrass is growing.

Listening For instance, livestock aren't allowed on most public lands, so farmers can remove the cheatgrass growing on their land, but they can't do anything about the public lands adjoining their property.

→ The professor disregards the suggestion in the reading passage that _____

_____ . She remarks that _____

_____ .

3 **Reading** It is also possible to remove cheatgrass through chemical means. Herbicides can be sprayed from backpack containers by individuals covering small areas, or they may be sprayed from motorized equipment or by crop dusters if there are particularly large infestations.

Listening As for herbicides . . . Well, they're effective only at certain times of the year, so they have to be properly managed. They're also expensive, and, you know, they harm the grasses and other plants growing alongside cheatgrass.

→ The professor further challenges the argument in the reading passage that _____

_____ .

D | Completing the Essay

Complete the following sample essay. Use the phrases to help you write your essay.

The professor and the author of the reading passage acknowledge that _____

_____ . Yet while the author of the reading passage suggests _____

_____ , the professor challenges _____ .

For example, the first proposal is to _____

_____ . The professor finds fault with these solutions though. She declares that _____

_____ . As for using fires,

she comments that _____

_____ .

The professor disregards the suggestion in the reading passage that _____

_____ . She remarks that _____

_____

_____ . What happens is that _____

_____ .

As for herbicides, the professor explains that _____ . She further

challenges the argument in the reading passage that _____

_____ .

In recent years, targeted grazing has become popular in certain areas. Essentially, herds of animals are used to control the growth of brush and weeds on tracts of land. Goats, which consume nearly every type of plant, are the most commonly used animals for this method of plant control, which first gained widespread media coverage in 2009 when the Internet company Google used a herd of goats to control the growth of brush on its grounds. These days, there are many businesses which rent herds of goats for targeted grazing.

One of the numerous advantages of targeted grazing is that it enables people to avoid using loud, gas-guzzling lawnmowers and other similar pieces of equipment, thereby reducing both noise and air pollution. Additionally, goats require no maintenance. In that way, they are unlike machines, which often break down and need repairing. Studies have additionally proven that renting a herd of goats is a cost-effective measure in comparison to using machinery for brush and grass cutting.

Goats are versatile brush and grass removers, too. They eat a wide variety of plants, especially weeds, which are troublesome to control. Thistle, blackberry, poison oak, poison ivy, and kudzu are merely a few of the plants which are resistant to traditional cutting methods and herbicides but which goats eat with relish. Furthermore, goats can climb up hillsides and over rocky terrain to eat brush that is difficult for machines and people to reach.

An additional benefit is that goats fertilize the ground while they are eating. They urinate and defecate on the ground, and both their urine and feces act as fertilizers when they are absorbed into the earth. Thus organic waste from the goats helps produce more plant life in an area soon after goats clear it.

A18

Directions You have 20 minutes to plan and write your response. Your response will be judged on the basis of the quality of your writing and on how well your response presents the points in the lecture and their relationship to the passage. Typically, an effective response will be 150-225 words.

Question Summarize the points made in the lecture, being sure to explain how they challenge specific claims made in the reading passage.

COPY   CUT   PASTE   **Word Count : 0**

A | Reading Passage

Read the following passage carefully. Try to understand what the main argument of the passage is.

In 1485, the English dynastic wars known as the Wars of the Roses concluded at the Battle of Bosworth Field when Henry Tudor's forces defeated those belonging to King Richard III. Richard himself was slain during the battle, and his body was buried alongside a church near what is the city of Leicester today. Over time, the location of his burial site was lost to history; however, in 2012, archaeologists exhumed a skeleton from beneath a carpark. Extensive testing, including DNA analysis, proved without a doubt that the body is that of Richard III.

To begin with, the skeleton is that of a man in his thirties, which was Richard's age when he was killed in battle. The body also has a noted curvature of the spine, an affliction Richard was known to have suffered. Furthermore, there is evidence of numerous head wounds, which correlates with reports from the battle regarding how Richard was killed.

Researchers at the University of Leicester tracked down two living descendants of Richard, both of whom belong to the family line of Anne, Richard's sister. Mitochondrial DNA extracted from the bones of the skeletal remains matched both of the subjects it was compared to. The DNA tests were conducted three times to make absolutely sure there were no mistakes.

Further testing using radiocarbon dating methods was done on the bones, and those tests indicated that the person was alive sometime between 1450 and 1540. Other tests showed that the person consumed a diet comprised mainly of seafood, exotic birds, and plenty of wine, indicating the person was someone of substance and certainly a member of the nobility. All of these factors led researchers to conclude that the skeleton was definitely that of King Richard III.

Vocabulary

- **dynastic** *adj* hereditary; successional
- **slay** *v* to kill
- **exhume** *v* to dig up from under the ground
- **skeleton** *n* a complete set of bones from a body
- **curvature** *n* a bending
- **spine** *n* a backbone
- **wound** *n* an injury, often severe in nature
- **correlate** *v* to match
- **descendant** *n* offspring; a person who descends from a specific ancestor
- **extract** *v* to remove; to take out
- **comprise** *v* to make up; to constitute
- **substance** *n* wealth; affluence

▚ Outlining

Write an outline of the reading passage in the space provided.

Main Point

Argument ❶

Argument ❷

Argument ❸

▚ Paraphrasing Exercises

Read the following sentences. Then, paraphrase them. Be sure to include the key information in each sentence.

1 There is evidence of numerous head wounds, which correlates with reports from the battle regarding how Richard was killed.

→

2 Mitochondrial DNA extracted from the bones of the skeletal remains matched both of the subjects it was compared to.

→

3 Other tests showed that the person consumed a diet comprised mainly of seafood, exotic birds, and plenty of wine, indicating the person was someone of substance and certainly a member of the nobility.

→

Listening Lecture 🎧 A19

Listen to a lecture on the topic you just read about. Be sure to take notes while you listen.

◪ Note-Taking

Main Point _____

_____

Argument ❶ _____

_____

Argument ❷ _____

_____

Argument ❸ _____

_____

◪ Paraphrasing Exercises

Read the following sentences. Then, paraphrase them. Be sure to include the key information in each sentence.

1 The curved spine might have resulted when the body was squeezed into the casket, which was tiny.

→ _____

_____

2 While the DNA from the bones matched the descendants of his sister Anne, it would also match the DNA of Richard's male cousins since they had the same grandmother.

→ _____

_____

3 While other tests proved the person ate foods rare for anyone other than nobles to consume, one of Richard's cousins would have eaten a similar diet.

→ _____

_____

C | Combining the Main Points

Read the following sentences from the reading passage and listening lecture. Then, combine each pair of sentences by using the given patterns.

1 **Reading** To begin with, the skeleton is that of a man in his thirties, which was Richard's age when he was killed in battle. The body also has a noted curvature of the spine, an affliction Richard was known to have suffered.

Listening These facts match what we know about Richard . . . but could also fit someone else. More than 1,000 people died in that battle, so it might not be Richard's body. Plus, the curved spine might have resulted when the body was squeezed into the casket, which was tiny.

→ **The professor starts by agreeing with the author of the reading passage that** _____

_____ **. Yet he says that** _____

_____ **.**

2 **Reading** Mitochondrial DNA extracted from the bones of the skeletal remains matched both of the subjects it was compared to.

Listening So while the DNA from the bones matched the descendants of his sister Anne, it would also match the DNA of Richard's male cousins since they had the same grandmother. So this could be the body of one of Richard's relatives, not Richard himself.

→ **Next, the professor admits that** _____

_____ **. However, he mentions the fact that** _____

_____ **.**

3 **Reading** Other tests showed that the person consumed a diet comprised mainly of seafood, exotic birds, and plenty of wine, indicating the person was someone of substance and certainly a member of the nobility.

Listening And while other tests proved the person ate foods rare for anyone other than nobles to consume, one of Richard's cousins would have eaten a similar diet.

→ **While the author of the reading passage believes** _____ **,**

the professor thinks _____ **.**

D | Completing the Essay

Complete the following sample essay. Use the phrases to help you write your essay.

During his lecture, the professor discusses _____ .

While the author of the reading passage believes that _____ ,

the professor brings up some points that _____ .

The professor starts by agreeing with the author of the reading passage that _____

_____ . Yet he says that _____

_____

_____ .

Next, the professor admits that _____

_____ . However, he mentions the fact that

_____

_____

_____ .

Lastly, the professor comments that _____ ,

and he also talks about _____ . While the author of the reading passage believes

_____ , the professor thinks _____

_____ .

In the middle of the fourteenth century, a devastating plague called the Black Death swept through parts of Asia and much of Europe. It originated in Asia around 1343, reached Eastern Europe by 1346, and by 1350, it had spread virtually everywhere in Europe, where it did not abate until 1352. It is estimated that between seventy-five and 100 million people died during that time. The Black Death had long-term negative economic, social, and religious impacts on society.

Economically, the Black Death destroyed the fabric of trade and the means of living for most Europeans. People were typically frightened to leave their homes unless it was absolutely necessary, so they failed to work. Fear of the illness led people to shun others, so strangers were treated with suspicion and were often barred from entering towns and villages. As a result, trade ground to a halt everywhere, resulting in goods becoming scarce and prices skyrocketing.

Socially, the fabric of society unraveled. Because people were afraid of coming into contact with others, many of the social aspects of life disappeared. Due to the high loss of life, farms were abandoned, and villages remained empty for many years afterward. There was a sense of hopelessness and a loss of faith in doctors and men of learning as they seemed to have no ideas regarding how to stop the plague from spreading.

As the Black Death continued killing people, the survivors turned to the church to save them. Much of the burden of caring for the sick fell upon priests, who, as a result, suffered a high rate of illness and death. When prayer subsequently failed, people lost faith in God and religion. This had a long-term negative effect because after the plague ended, people began indulging themselves in living lives of pleasure.

A20

Directions You have 20 minutes to plan and write your response. Your response will be judged on the basis of the quality of your writing and on how well your response presents the points in the lecture and their relationship to the passage. Typically, an effective response will be 150-225 words.

Question Summarize the points made in the lecture, being sure to explain how they challenge specific arguments made in the reading passage.

COPY	CUT	PASTE	Word Count : 0

Part B

Independent Writing Task

Independent Writing Task

◢ About the Question

The Independent Writing Task requires you to read a question and then to write an essay about the question. Many questions present a statement and ask you if you agree or disagree with it. You should then choose and write an essay expressing your opinion. Other questions present you with a situation and two choices. You should select one and then write your essay. Recently, some questions present you with a situation and provide you with three choices. You should select one of the three and then write your essay. You will be given 30 minutes to write your essay. Your essay should be more than 300 words. Try to make your essay between 300 and 400 words. That will be long enough to provide enough examples and short enough to give you plenty of time to proofread your essay when you finish it. The ideal essay has an introduction, a body, and a conclusion. The introduction should describe your opinion. The body should contain either two or three paragraphs that present separate points or arguments. It is more common to use three separate points or arguments than two. Be sure to provide examples to support your arguments. And the conclusion should summarize the points that you made in the body.

There are three possible writing tasks you will be presented with, but they all ask you to express your opinion about an important issue.

For the agree/disagree type, the task will be presented in the following way:

- Do you agree or disagree with the following statement?
  [*A sentence or sentences that present an issue*]
  Use specific reasons and examples to support your answer.

  cf. This question type accounts for most of the essay topics that have been asked on the TOEFL® iBT so far.

For the preference type, the task will be presented in the following way:

- Some people prefer X. Others prefer Y. Which do you prefer? Use specific reasons and examples to support your choice.

For the opinion type, the task will be presented in the following way:

- [*A sentence or sentences that state a fact*]
  In your opinion, what is one thing that should be . . . ? Use specific reasons and examples to support your answer.

▮ Sample Question

Directions   Read the question below. You have 30 minutes to plan, write, and revise your essay. Typically, an effective response will contain a minimum of 300 words.

Question   Do you agree or disagree with the following statement?

Family members ought to spend time together every evening.

Use specific reasons and examples to support your answer.

Sample Essay

I strongly agree with the statement because I believe it is important for family members to spend time together every evening. There are three main reasons why I believe this.

Firstly, family members who spend time together on a regular basis can become closer. This will enable them to understand one another, to get along better, and to become more interested in one another's lives. No matter how busy we are, everyone in my family spends time together each evening. We have dinner together and then talk together in the family room. We started doing this three years ago, and our relationships have grown much stronger. Previously, we argued constantly and got into fights. We also did not care much about our other family members. Now, the exact opposite situation exists. We get along very well and are deeply concerned about the lives of everyone in our family.

Another benefit of spending time together regularly is that we can talk about our day's activities. This lets us discuss what we did and how it worked out for us. Last night, I told my family about my baseball game and how I had performed in it. Then, my sister talked about her performance on an exam, and my parents described their days at their jobs. It was a great opportunity for us to learn more about everyone's life and what was happening.

A third advantage is that we can make plans for the future. When we spend time together on the weekend, my parents often tell us what is going to happen in the coming week. Furthermore, my sister and I discuss what we are planning to do at our schools and in our private lives. My parents take notes so that they can help remind us about any school assignments or projects we have to work on. This helps my sister and me be much better organized than our friends, who do not do anything like this.

I fully agree with the statement that family members should spend time together every evening. By doing so, they can forge closer relationships, talk about their daily activities, and discuss their plans for the future. All three of those actions can help make people's lives much better.

Chapter 01

A | Brainstorming

Read the question below and brainstorm your ideas.

Question

Do you agree or disagree with the following statement?

The success of a school depends upon its teachers.

Use specific reasons and examples to support your answer.

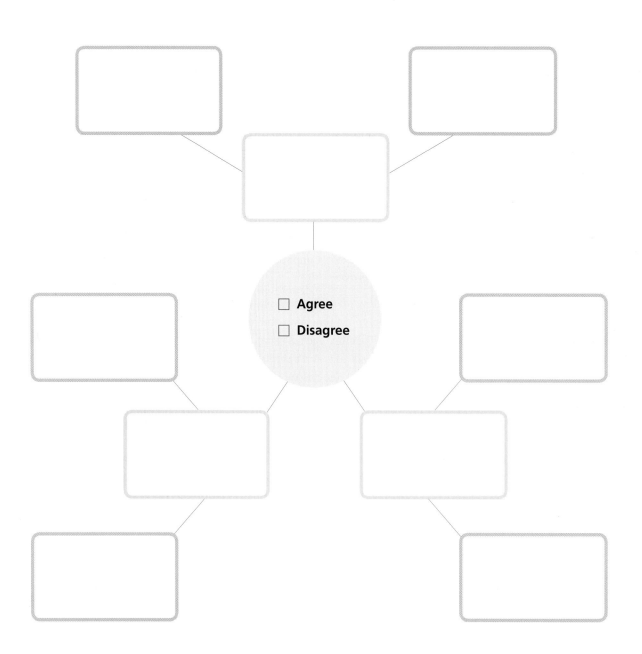

☐ **Agree**

☐ **Disagree**

B | Outlining

Complete the following outline based on your brainstorming map.

Thesis Statement

First Supporting Idea

Topic Sentence:

Supporting Example(s):

Second Supporting Idea

Topic Sentence:

Supporting Example(s):

Third Supporting Idea

Topic Sentence:

Supporting Example(s):

Conclusion

C | Completing the Essay

Complete the following sample essay. Use the phrases to help you write your essay.

Agree

I agree with this statement. In my opinion, _____

_____

The first reason is very simple. _____

_____

_____

_____

_____

A second reason teachers are important is that _____

_____

_____

_____

_____

A third reason is that _____

_____

_____

_____

_____

_____

Teachers are clearly of great importance to the success of a school. _____

_____

_____

I believe teachers are important to schools, but I do not agree with the statement.

First of all,

Another reason is that

Finally,

I disagree with the statement because

iBT Practice Test

> **Directions** Read the question below. You have 30 minutes to plan, write, and revise your essay. Typically, an effective response will contain a minimum of 300 words.

Question Do you agree or disagree with the following statement?

It is important for the elderly to study and learn new things.

Use specific reasons and examples to support your answer.

COPY   CUT   PASTE   Word Count : 0

VOLUME HELP NEXT

HIDE TIME 00:20:00

Chapter 02

A | Brainstorming

Read the question below and brainstorm your ideas.

> **Question**
>
> These days, people use the Internet to work, to study, to communicate with others, and to be entertained. Being online is vital to the lives of people around the world. However, Internet access can be too expensive for many people to afford.
>
> Do you agree or disagree that the government, not individuals, should pay for the Internet? Why? Use specific reasons and examples to support your answer.

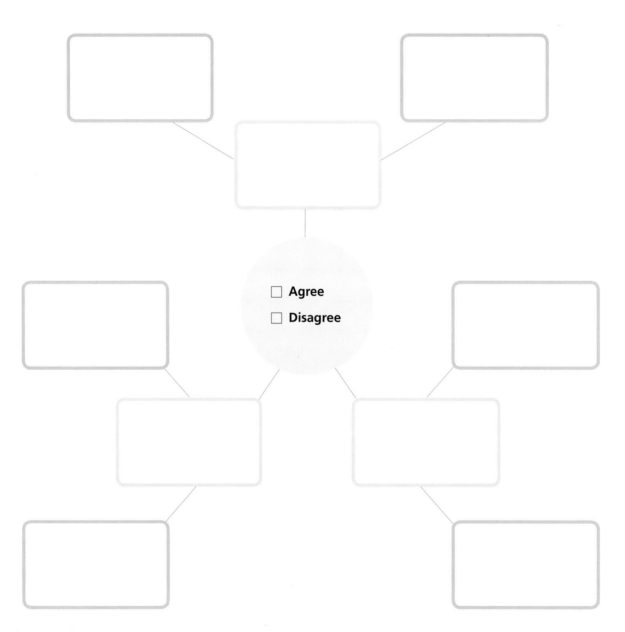

B | Outlining

Complete the following outline based on your brainstorming map.

Thesis Statement

First Supporting Idea

Topic Sentence:

Supporting Example(s):

Second Supporting Idea

Topic Sentence:

Supporting Example(s):

Third Supporting Idea

Topic Sentence:

Supporting Example(s):

Conclusion

C Completing the Essay

Complete the following sample essay. Use the phrases to help you write your essay.

Agree

I believe that _____

_____

The first reason is that _____

_____

_____

_____

_____

Furthermore, I believe _____

_____

_____

_____

_____

The final issue is that _____

_____

_____

_____

_____

It is clear to me that _____

_____

_____

_____

Disagree

While I understand why people might support having the government pay for access to the

Internet, _____

_____ I feel this way for a few reasons.

One is that _____

_____

_____

_____

_____

A second reason is that _____

_____

_____

_____

_____

Lastly, _____

_____

_____

_____

_____

The government should not pay for people to access the Internet since _____

_____

_____

_____

Directions Read the question below. You have 30 minutes to plan, write, and revise your essay. Typically, an effective response will contain a minimum of 300 words.

Question Do you agree or disagree with the following statement?

In order to attract more tourists, the government should pay to improve the appearances of old buildings and streets.

Use specific reasons and examples to support your answer.

COPY	CUT	PASTE		Word Count : 0

A Brainstorming

Read the question below and brainstorm your ideas.

Question

Sometimes companies cause damage to the environment due to the goods or services that they provide. Some people believe heavy fines need to be imposed upon these companies. Others think there are different ways to punish them. Which would you prefer? Use specific reasons and examples to support your answer.

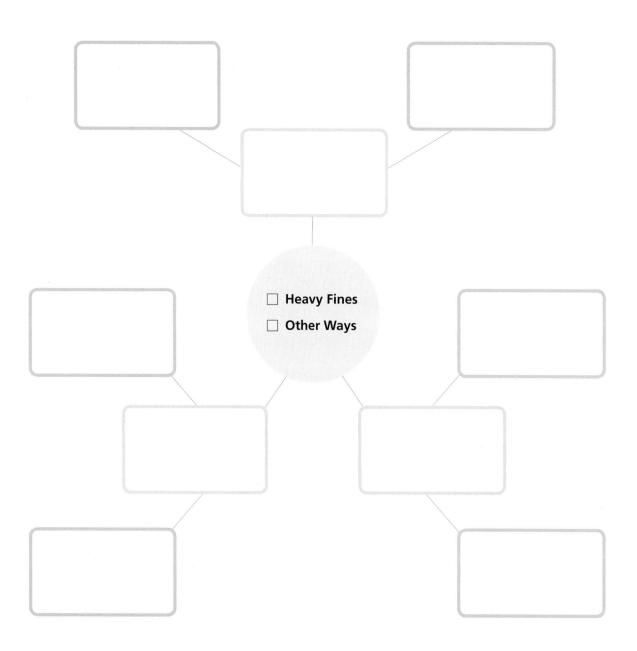

☐ **Heavy Fines**
☐ **Other Ways**

B | Outlining

Complete the following outline based on your brainstorming map.

Thesis Statement

First Supporting Idea

Topic Sentence:

Supporting Example(s):

Second Supporting Idea

Topic Sentence:

Supporting Example(s):

Third Supporting Idea

Topic Sentence:

Supporting Example(s):

Conclusion

C Completing the Essay

Complete the following sample essay. Use the phrases to help you write your essay.

Heavy Fines

When a company harms the environment through the goods or services it sells, it must be punished.

The first reason is that _____

_____

_____

_____

_____

When the government fines a company for the harm it causes the environment, _____

_____

_____

_____

_____

A final point is that _____

_____

_____

_____

_____

For those reasons, I consider fines to be the best form of punishment for companies that harm the environment.

Other Ways

While fines can be a useful means of punishment, there are other ways to deal with companies that harm the environment. _____

The first method of punishment I support is _____

_____

_____

_____

_____

_____

Next, _____

_____

_____

_____

_____

Finally, _____

_____

_____

_____

_____

It is obvious that there are better ways of punishing those who cause damage to the environment than fines. _____

_____

Directions   Read the question below. You have 30 minutes to plan, write, and revise your essay. Typically, an effective response will contain a minimum of 300 words.

Question The Earth's supply of fossil fuels is quickly declining as people are using coal, oil, and gas more than ever for their energy needs. Some people believe we should conserve energy by raising the prices of gasoline and electricity. Others think we ought to spend more money developing alternative forms of energy. Which would you prefer? Use specific reasons and examples to support your answer.

| COPY | CUT | PASTE | Word Count : 0 |

A | Brainstorming

Read the question below and brainstorm your ideas.

Question

A university has been supporting students financially so that they can do various extracurricular activities. This year, due to a lack of funds, the university can support only one activity. Which activity should the university support, sports, art, or volunteering? Use specific reasons and examples to support your answer.

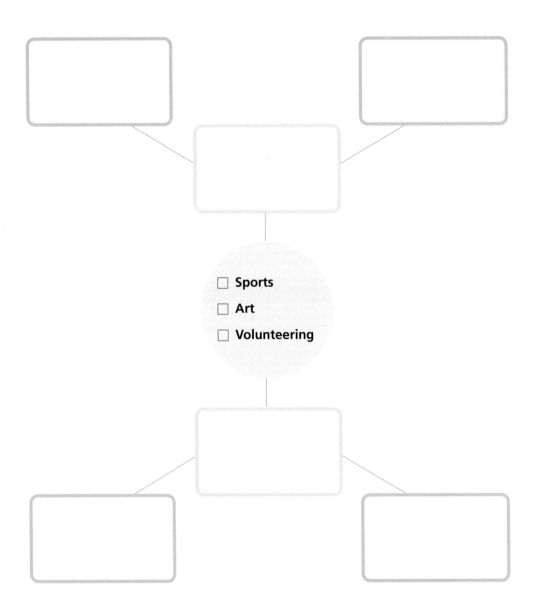

☐ Sports

☐ Art

☐ Volunteering

B Outlining

Complete the following outline based on your brainstorming map.

Thesis Statement

First Supporting Idea

Topic Sentence:

Supporting Example(s):

Second Supporting Idea

Topic Sentence:

Supporting Example(s):

Conclusion

C Completing the Essay

Complete the following sample essay. Use the phrases to help you write your essay.

Sports

It is unfortunate that the university is suffering from a lack of funds and can only support one activity since each of them is worthy. But because a choice must be made, _____

_____

The first reason is that _____

_____

_____

_____

_____

_____

_____

Universities are not only places where students go to improve their minds, but they are also places where they can improve their bodies. _____

_____

_____

_____

_____

_____

_____

I wish the school could provide funding for all three activities, but since it cannot, the choice is clear:

_____

_____

Art

The university has a tough choice to make. It must choose between supporting sports, art, and volunteering. I like all three options, but I believe _____

_____

One reason is that _____

_____

_____

_____

_____

_____

Another factor to consider is that _____

_____

_____

_____

_____

_____

_____

In my opinion, _____

_____

_____

Directions Read the question below. You have 30 minutes to plan, write, and revise your essay. Typically, an effective response will contain a minimum of 300 words.

Question A school is requiring its students to do some community service this year. They can clean a park, plant flowers and trees, or help build a bicycle path. Which activity would you prefer? Use specific reasons and examples to support your answer.

COPY   CUT   PASTE   Word Count : 0

Chapter 05

A Brainstorming

Read the question below and brainstorm your ideas.

> **Question**
>
> Do you agree or disagree with the following statement?
>
> **In order to succeed in life, it is better to be similar to other people than to be different from them.**
>
> Use specific reasons and examples to support your answer.

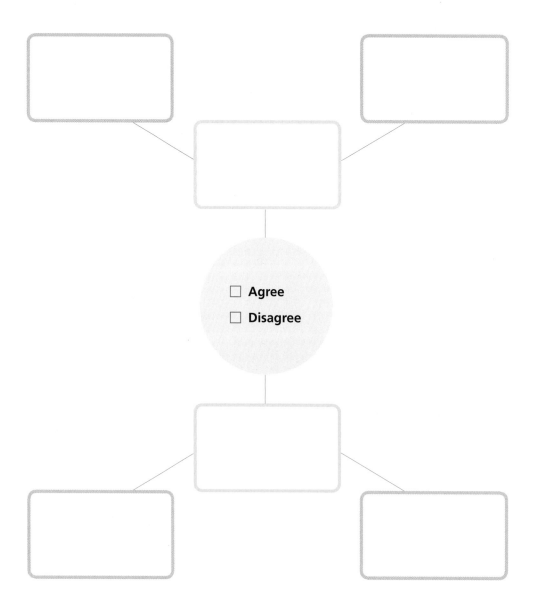

☐ Agree
☐ Disagree

B | Outlining

Complete the following outline based on your brainstorming map.

Thesis Statement

First Supporting Idea

Topic Sentence:

Supporting Example(s):

Second Supporting Idea

Topic Sentence:

Supporting Example(s):

Conclusion

C | Completing the Essay

Complete the following sample essay. Use the phrases to help you write your essay.

Agree

_____

_____

_____ , so I must agree with the statement.

In my culture, _____

_____

_____

_____

_____

_____

_____

Another way that being similar to others leads to success is that _____

_____

_____

_____

_____

_____

It is clear to me that _____

_____

_____

Disagree

_____

_____ , Consequently, I find myself in disagreement with the statement.

Today, one of the easiest ways for a person to succeed in life is to _____

There are also _____

I therefore do not believe that the statement is correct, so I disagree with it.

> **Directions**   Read the question below. You have 30 minutes to plan, write, and revise your essay. Typically, an effective response will contain a minimum of 300 words.

Question Do you agree or disagree with the following statement?

A great leader should listen to the opinions of other people.

Use specific reasons and examples to support your answer.

COPY   CUT   PASTE   Word Count : 0

A | Brainstorming

Read the question below and brainstorm your ideas.

Question

Some people believe that older siblings should take care of their younger siblings. Others think that the children's parents should look after them. What do you think? Use specific reasons and examples to support your answer.

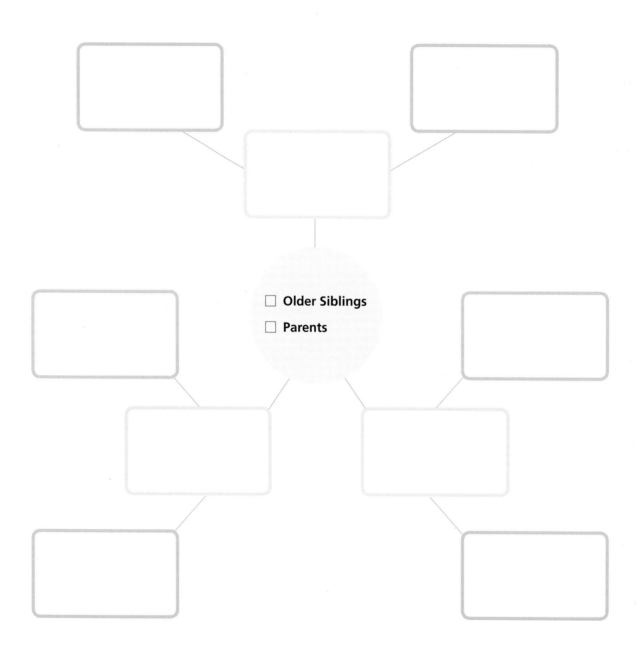

☐ **Older Siblings**
☐ **Parents**

B | Outlining

Complete the following outline based on your brainstorming map.

Thesis Statement

First Supporting Idea

Topic Sentence:

Supporting Example(s):

Second Supporting Idea

Topic Sentence:

Supporting Example(s):

Third Supporting Idea

Topic Sentence:

Supporting Example(s):

Conclusion

C | Completing the Essay

Complete the following sample essay. Use the phrases to help you write your essay.

Older Siblings

I imagine that the majority of people would say that parents ought to take care of their young children.

One reason I feel this way is that

Another reason is that

A final reason is that

Older siblings, not parents, should be responsible for taking care of their younger siblings.

I have seen older siblings trying to take care of their younger brothers and sisters, and their efforts seldom ended in success.

The first reason is the most obvious one:

Additionally, when parents take care of their children,

Yet another advantage of having parents raise their young children is that

For those three reasons, I think that it is better for children to be raised by their parents rather than by their younger siblings.

Directions Read the question below. You have 30 minutes to plan, write, and revise your essay. Typically, an effective response will contain a minimum of 300 words.

Question Some people think that children should move out of their parents' homes after they graduate from high school. Others believe that children should continue to live with their parents until they get married. What do you think? Use specific reasons and examples to support your answer.

COPY   CUT   PASTE   Word Count : 0

HIDE TIME 00:20:00

A Brainstorming

Read the question below and brainstorm your ideas.

Question

Some students prefer to do their homework after school. Others prefer to be allowed to choose to do other activities. Which would you prefer? Use specific reasons and examples to support your answer.

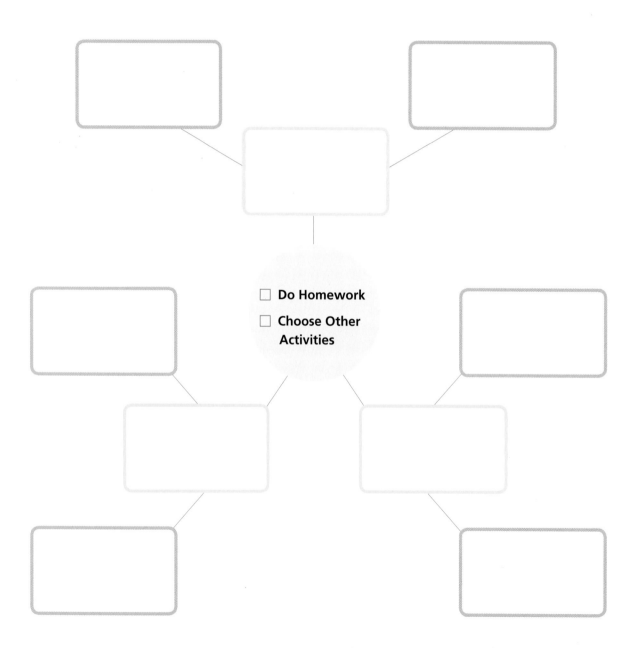

☐ Do Homework

☐ Choose Other Activities

B Outlining

Complete the following outline based on your brainstorming map.

Thesis Statement

First Supporting Idea

Topic Sentence:

Supporting Example(s):

Second Supporting Idea

Topic Sentence:

Supporting Example(s):

Third Supporting Idea

Topic Sentence:

Supporting Example(s):

Conclusion

C | Completing the Essay

Complete the following sample essay. Use the phrases to help you write your essay.

Do Homework

As long as people are in school, they should do their homework after school is done for the day. _____

_____

_____

Homework is an integral part of the education process, so students can _____

_____

_____

_____

_____

Doing homework can also help students _____

_____

_____

_____

_____

_____

Students can learn a great deal about _____

_____

_____

_____

_____

While I do not always enjoy doing homework, I appreciate how important it is, so I believe _____

_____

In my opinion, students should not be forced to do their homework after school but

I am a big supporter of

We should also consider that not all students

Parents should remember that students

Not all students like school or do well at it, so they should be allowed to

iBT Practice Test

Directions Read the question below. You have 30 minutes to plan, write, and revise your essay. Typically, an effective response will contain a minimum of 300 words.

Question An elementary school has been given some extra funds to spend on its students this year. It can use the money to improve the quality of food in the cafeteria, or it can pay for students to participate in extracurricular activities after school ends. Which would you prefer? Use specific reasons and examples to support your answer.

| COPY | CUT | PASTE | | Word Count : 0 |

A | Brainstorming

Read the question below and brainstorm your ideas.

Question

Do you agree or disagree with the following statement?

It is better to have an intelligent friend than a friend with a good sense of humor.

Use specific reasons and examples to support your answer.

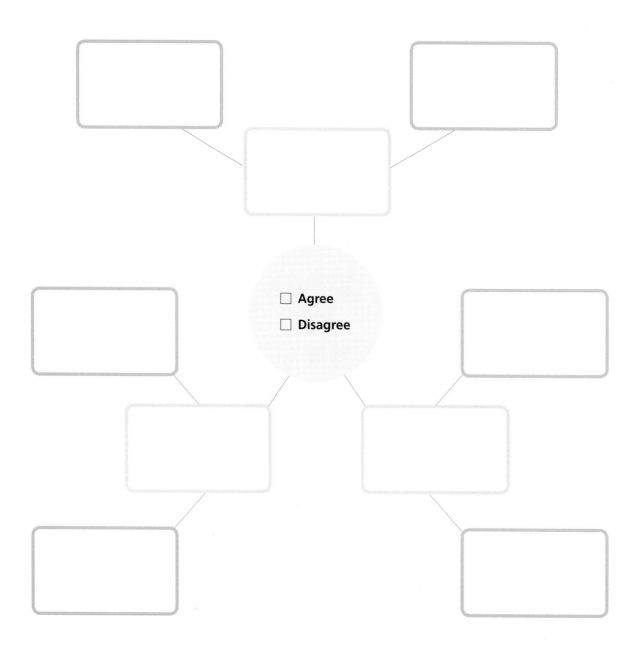

☐ Agree
☐ Disagree

B | Outlining

Complete the following outline based on your brainstorming map.

Thesis Statement

First Supporting Idea

Topic Sentence:

Supporting Example(s):

Second Supporting Idea

Topic Sentence:

Supporting Example(s):

Third Supporting Idea

Topic Sentence:

Supporting Example(s):

Conclusion

C | Completing the Essay

Complete the following sample essay. Use the phrases to help you write your essay.

Agree

It might be fun to have a friend with a good sense of humor, but _____
_____
_____

The first reason is that _____
_____
_____
_____
_____
_____

Furthermore, _____
_____
_____
_____
_____
_____

Finally, _____
_____
_____
_____
_____

An intelligent friend is better to have than a friend with a good sense of humor. _____
_____
_____

Disagree

It might be nice to have an intelligent friend, but

A friend with a sense of humor can

A second advantage to having a friend with a sense of humor is that

Funny friends are

A friend with a sense of humor is much better than an intelligent friend.

iBT Practice Test

> **Directions** Read the question below. You have 30 minutes to plan, write, and revise your essay. Typically, an effective response will contain a minimum of 300 words.

Question Do you agree or disagree with the following statement?

People can learn many things from their friends.

Use specific reasons and examples to support your answer.

COPY	CUT	PASTE	Word Count : 0

A | Brainstorming

Read the question below and brainstorm your ideas.

Question

Do you agree or disagree with the following statement?

Teachers should use video games in classes with children ages five to eight to help them become more interested in certain topics.

Use specific reasons and examples to support your answer.

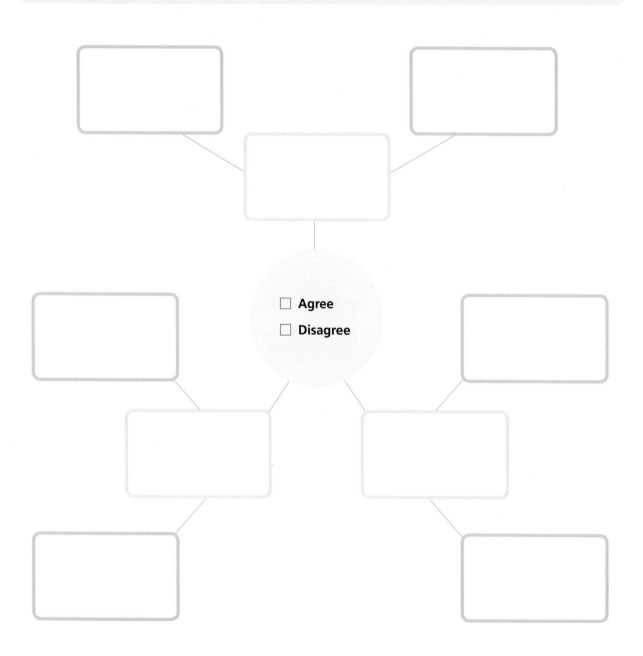

☐ **Agree**
☐ **Disagree**

B | Outlining

Complete the following outline based on your brainstorming map.

Thesis Statement

First Supporting Idea

Topic Sentence:

Supporting Example(s):

Second Supporting Idea

Topic Sentence:

Supporting Example(s):

Third Supporting Idea

Topic Sentence:

Supporting Example(s):

Conclusion

C | Completing the Essay

Complete the following sample essay. Use the phrases to help you write your essay.

Agree

Video games can definitely help children between the ages of five to eight learn because _____

_____

_____

Most children have a hard time paying attention to their teachers in class, but they love video games,

so _____

_____

_____

_____

Nowadays, _____

_____

_____

_____

Most elementary school students do the same thing every day: _____

_____

_____

_____

_____

Teachers ought to use video games to teach students who are between five and eight years of age. ___

_____

_____

_____

It seems like it would be fun to teach young students by using video games, but _____

_____

The main reason is that _____

_____

_____

_____

_____

Another problem is that _____

_____

_____

_____

_____

Once students are permitted to play games as a part of their learning experience, they _____

_____

_____

_____

_____

It would be a huge mistake for teachers to use video games to teach young students. _____

_____

_____

_____

Directions Read the question below. You have 30 minutes to plan, write, and revise your essay. Typically, an effective response will contain a minimum of 300 words.

Question Governments and private individuals sometimes contribute large amounts of money to various universities. However, rather than spending the money to make improvements that would benefit the entire student body, universities often choose instead to hire famous lecturers who appeal only to a small minority of students.

Do you agree or disagree that universities should invest more money in their facilities, such as libraries and science laboratories, than on hiring famous lecturers? Use specific reasons and examples to support your answer.

COPY	CUT	PASTE				Word Count : 0

A | Brainstorming

Read the question below and brainstorm your ideas.

Question

Do you agree or disagree with the following statement?

It is better to spend money by going on a trip than to save it for the future.

Use specific reasons and examples to support your answer.

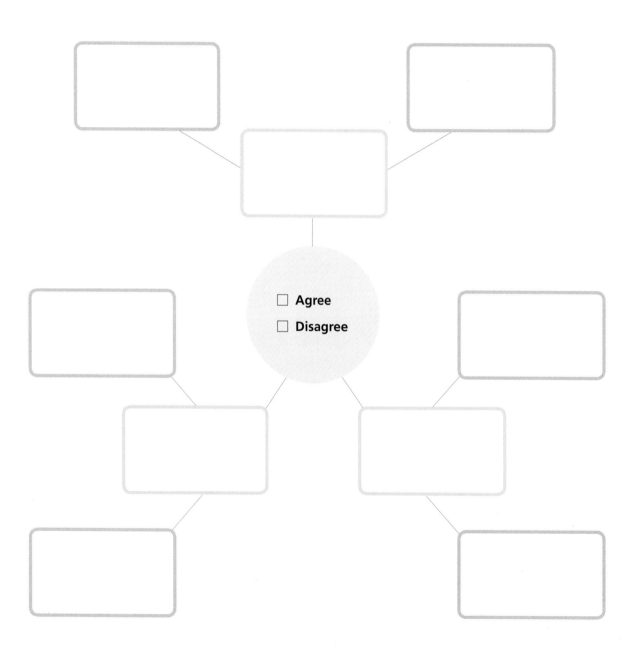

B | Outlining

Complete the following outline based on your brainstorming map.

Thesis Statement

First Supporting Idea

Topic Sentence:

Supporting Example(s):

Second Supporting Idea

Topic Sentence:

Supporting Example(s):

Third Supporting Idea

Topic Sentence:

Supporting Example(s):

Conclusion

C Completing the Essay

Complete the following sample essay. Use the phrases to help you write your essay.

Agree

If a person has the opportunity to go on a trip, that individual ought to do that instead of merely saving the money to use in the future. _____

The first reason is that _____

_____

_____

_____

_____

The second reason is that _____

_____

_____

_____

_____

_____

A third reason is that _____

_____

_____

_____

_____

_____

I fully agree with the statement. _____

_____

_____

Disagree

While taking a trip can be fun, I disagree with the statement. I believe the opposite and think that

These days, too many people focus

In addition, too many people waste money

Something else to consider is that

I disagree with the statement because I believe

Directions Read the question below. You have 30 minutes to plan, write, and revise your essay. Typically, an effective response will contain a minimum of 300 words.

Question Do you agree or disagree with the following statement?

Playing sports can teach people important lessons about life.

Use specific reasons and examples to support your answer.

COPY   CUT   PASTE   Word Count : 0

Actual Test

Writing Section Directions

 Make sure your headset is on.

This section measures your ability to use writing to communicate in an academic environment. There will be two writing tasks.

For the first writing task, you will read a passage and listen to a lecture and then answer a question based on what you have read and heard. For the second writing task, you will answer a question based on your own knowledge and experience.

Now listen to the directions for the first writing task.

Writing Based on Reading and Listening

For this task, you will first have **3 minutes** to read a passage about an academic topic. You may take notes on the passage if you wish. The passage will then be removed and you will listen to a lecture about the same topic. While you listen, you may also take notes.

Then you will have **20 minutes** to write a response to a question that asks you about the relationship between the lecture you heard and the reading passage. Try to answer the question as completely as possible using information from the reading passage and the lecture. The question does **not** ask you to express your personal opinion. You will be able to see the reading passage again when it is time for you to write. You may use your notes to help you answer the question.

Typically, an effective response will be 150 to 225 words long. Your response will be judged on the quality of your writing and on the completeness and accuracy of the content. If you finish your response before the the time is up, you may click on **NEXT** to go on to the second writing task.

Now you will see the reading passage for 3 minutes. Remember it will be available to you again when you are writing. Immediately after the reading time ends, the lecture will begin, so keep your headset on until the lecture is over.

Sick employees and those suffering from chronic health problems are burdens to their companies because the loss of work hours results in lower productivity by workers and fewer profits for businesses. One way that companies can reduce the effects of these problems is to offer health incentive plans. They may offer monetary incentives to workers who take fewer sick days off. They may also provide in-house exercise facilities and give bonuses to those employees who regularly utilize them, and they may further encourage healthy living by bestowing financial awards or other types of compensation upon individuals who lose weight or quit smoking.

Programs such as these have several advantages, one of which is that they encourage workers—especially those lacking motivation—to become healthier. By offering rewards for improved health and taking fewer sick days, companies can inspire their employees to become healthier. These healthy workers become happy and more productive.

Additionally, these inducements are effective on those who are already fit, do not smoke, and lack other bad habits simply by encouraging them to maintain their healthy lifestyles. Rather than giving monetary rewards, companies may provide incentives such as lower health insurance rates and longer periods of vacation to convince their employees to stay in shape for long periods of time.

The ultimate goals of these programs are to save money on expenditures and to increase profits. For every day an employee is out sick, a company loses money, and those workers who end up suffering long-term health problems due to unhealthy lifestyles regularly have their health care subsidized by their employers, which can be expensive. Thus companies can save money by ensuring that their workers are as healthy as possible.

🎧 AT01

Directions You have 20 minutes to plan and write your response. Your response will be judged on the basis of the quality of your writing and on how well your response presents the points in the lecture and their relationship to the passage. Typically, an effective response will be 150-225 words.

Question Summarize the points made in the lecture, being sure to explain how they cast doubt on specific points made in the reading passage.

COPY CUT PASTE Word Count : 0

Sick employees and those suffering from chronic health problems are burdens to their companies because the loss of work hours results in lower productivity by workers and fewer profits for businesses. One way that companies can reduce the effects of these problems is to offer health incentive plans. They may offer monetary incentives to workers who take fewer sick days off. They may also provide in-house exercise facilities and give bonuses to those employees who regularly utilize them, and they may further encourage healthy living by bestowing financial awards or other types of compensation upon individuals who lose weight or quit smoking.

Programs such as these have several advantages, one of which is that they encourage workers—especially those lacking motivation—to become healthier. By offering rewards for improved health and taking fewer sick days, companies can inspire their employees to become healthier. These healthy workers become happy and more productive.

Additionally, these inducements are effective on those who are already fit, do not smoke, and lack other bad habits simply by encouraging them to maintain their healthy lifestyles. Rather than giving monetary rewards, companies may provide incentives such as lower health insurance rates and longer periods of vacation to convince their employees to stay in shape for long periods of time.

The ultimate goals of these programs are to save money on expenditures and to increase profits. For every day an employee is out sick, a company loses money, and those workers who end up suffering long-term health problems due to unhealthy lifestyles regularly have their health care subsidized by their employers, which can be expensive. Thus companies can save money by ensuring that their workers are as healthy as possible.

Writing Based on Knowledge and Experience

For this task, you will write an essay in response to a question that asks you to state, explain, and support your opinion on an issue. You have **30 minutes** to write your essay.

Typically, an effective essay will contain a minimum of 300 words. Your essay will be judged on the quality of your writing. This includes the development of your ideas, the organization of the content, and the quality and accuracy of the language you used to express ideas.

Click on **CONTINUE** to go on.

COPY   CUT   PASTE   Word Count : 0

Directions Read the question below. You have 30 minutes to plan, write, and revise your essay. Typically, an effective response will contain a minimum of 300 words.

Question

Do you agree or disagree with the following statement?

It is important for schools and businesses to have rules regarding the types of clothing that people are allowed to wear.

Use specific reasons and examples to support your answer.

Authors

Michael A. Putlack

- MA in History, Tufts University, Medford, MA, USA
- Expert test developer of TOEFL, TOEIC, and TEPS
- Main author of the Darakwon *How to Master Skills for the TOEFL® iBT* series and *TOEFL® MAP* series

Stephen Poirier

- Candidate for PhD in History, University of Western Ontario, Canada
- Certificate of Professional Technical Writing, Carleton University, Canada
- Co-author of the Darakwon *How to Master Skills for the TOEFL® iBT* series and *TOEFL® MAP* series

Decoding the **TOEFL**® iBT
WRITING Advanced NEW TOEFL® EDITION

Publisher Chung Kyudo
Editor Kim Minju
Authors Michael A. Putlack, Stephen Poirier
Proofreader Michael A. Putlack
Designers Koo Soojung, Park Sunyoung

First published in October 2021
By Darakwon, Inc.
Darakwon Bldg., 211, Munbal-ro, Paju-si, Gyeonggi-do 10881
Republic of Korea
Tel: 82-2-736-2031 (Ext. 250)
Fax: 82-2-732-2037

Price ₩18,000
ISBN 978-89-277-0887-2 14740
         978-89-277-0875-9 14740 (set)

www.darakwon.co.kr

Components Student Book / Answer Book
7 6 5 4 3 2 1   21 22 23 24 25

Decoding the TOEFL® iBT

Scripts
Answers
Sample Essays

Advanced

WRITING

Decoding the TOEFL® iBT

Advanced

WRITING

Scripts
Answers
Sample Essays

Chapter 01

A | Reading Passage
p. 16

Outlining

<u>Main Point: emerald ash tree borer = invasive species causing problems by killing trees in U.S. and Canada</u>

Argument 1: stop sending infected wood to other regions = prevent larvae from moving elsewhere
- are laws banning ash wood from being shipped to other places

Argument 2: use insecticides → inject into trees
- can kill insects for up to 3 years

Argument 3: propose introducing new insects from Asia
- insects consume ash tree borer larvae = can eradicate them

Paraphrasing Exercises

1 There are laws in some areas banning ash wood being shipped elsewhere so that the insects cannot move to other places.

2 The insecticide in an ash tree can kill pests for up to three years.

3 It might be possible to control or kill the emerald ash tree borer by importing these harmless insects to North America.

B | Listening Lecture
p. 18

Listening Script

Now listen to part of a lecture on the topic you just read about.

W Professor: The insect on the screen is the emerald ash tree borer. It has been in the news lately because it's spreading across the eastern part of North America and is causing hundreds of millions of dollars in damage to the forests there. The larvae of this insect dig into ash trees, destroy their bark, and cause the trees to die. While some measures have been implemented and others proposed, unfortunately, they're all problematic for various reasons.

Lately, the government has been attempting to halt the spread of the insect by banning ash wood from being shipped, uh, even as firewood. Nowadays, ash wood harvested in a region must remain there. This method has problems though. First, it's costing logging companies large sums of money, and second, it's not really effective anyway. You see, uh, the insect has wings and can fly. So flying from place to place is one of the ways the emerald ash borer has been spreading. Halting log shipments simply won't work.

Insecticides are currently being applied directly to ash trees, but doing this comes with its own set of problems. Basically, there are too many ash trees. Sure, um, you can use insecticides on the ash trees in your yard, but what about when there are tens of thousands of ash trees in a single forest . . . ? Using insecticides would require excessive manpower and money, so it's not a practical option.

Some have suggested importing new insects from Asia to control the spread of the emerald ash borer. That's a horrible idea. We don't need more invasive species in the country. Who knows what harm they could cause? Sure, people say these other insects are harmless, yet we simply can't anticipate what damage a new species can do when it's introduced into an environment where it has no natural enemies.

Note-Taking

<u>Main Point: all ways of stopping emerald ash tree borer have problems</u>

Argument 1: banning ash trees from being shipped = costs logging companies money
- not effective since insect has wings and can fly

Argument 2: can use insecticide in yards but can't apply in forests with many trees
- requires too much manpower and money

Argument 3: importing new insects from Asia = horrible idea
- would be invasive species so could cause great harm

Paraphrasing Exercises

1 The government is trying to stop the insect from moving elsewhere by banning the shipping of ash wood.

2 Using insecticides is impractical due to the high costs in time and money.

3 Despite claims that the insects are harmless, nobody knows what damage they can do in a place where they have no natural enemies.

C | Combining the Main Points
p. 19

1 In mentioning that <u>the insect can spread easily since it can fly</u>, the professor contradicts the assertion in the reading passage that <u>laws banning the shipping of ash wood will stop the spread of the insect</u>.

2 The reading passage claims that <u>insecticides injected into</u>

ash trees can kill insects for up to three years. While the professor admits that insecticides are effective, she points out that a single forest may contain an enormous number of ash trees.

3   The author of the reading passage argues that three different harmless species could be introduced to North America to kill the insect, but the professor notes that nobody knows what damage these species could cause.

D | Completing the Essay   p. 20

Sample Essay

The professor lectures about the emerald ash tree borer, an invasive species of insect that is killing ash trees in eastern North America. In her talk, the professor challenges all three solutions which are presented in the reading passage.

First, the professor disputes the notion that laws requiring ash trees infected by the emerald ash tree borer to remain in the places they were cut down are effective. In mentioning that the insect can spread easily since it can fly, the professor contradicts the assertion in the reading passage that laws banning the shipping of ash wood will stop the spread of the insect.

Next, the reading passage claims that insecticides injected into ash trees can kill insects for up to three years. While the professor admits that insecticides are effective, she points out that a single forest may contain an enormous number of ash trees. Therefore, protecting every ash tree with insecticides will require a lot of time and money, so it is not feasible.

Finally, the professor strongly disagrees with the suggestion to use other invasive species to kill the emerald ash tree borer. The author of the reading passage argues that three different harmless species could be introduced to North America to kill the insect, but the professor notes that nobody knows what damage these species could cause.

iBT Practice Test   p. 21

Sample Notes — READING

Texas wild rice = being threatened w/extinction but may be saved

1   **water level of San Marcos River = lowered**
   –   trying to reduce river water used + people requested not to waste water

2   **nutria consumes rice plants**
   –   culling nutria by paying people to hunt and kill it
   –   scientists working on pesticide to kill it but no other animals or plants

3   **people using lake for recreation harm plant**
   –   inform people about plant = don't hit with boats, swim near it, or dislodge
   –   advise boaters not to cause pollution

Listening Script

Now listen to part of a lecture on the topic you just read about.

M Professor: Without a doubt, someday soon, Texas wild rice will become extinct, uh, at least in the wild. While some plants are grown in university laboratories, it's estimated there are fewer than 200 plants remaining by the San Marcos River in southeastern Texas. While attempts are being made to save it, I, uh, I don't like the plant's chances of surviving.

Why is that . . . ? Well, the plant requires copious amounts of water, but the water in the San Marcos River is being depleted. The river is being drained and dammed, so less water is flowing through it, which means that the rice can't survive. Efforts being made to reduce water usage are futile, too, since the local population is growing. There have been some droughts as well, thereby further reducing the water level.

Another problem concerns the nutria, which is, uh, basically a large water rat. It chews rice stalks and often digs up the plants by their roots and eats them, which kills the plants. Efforts to hunt the nutria aren't effective since it breeds so quickly. Females, you see, can give birth to three litters a year. And pesticides have limited effects since most aren't effective against the nutria.

Human actions, such as polluting the San Marcos River and irresponsible boating, are further killing the rice plants. Pollution can't be controlled easily because chemical fertilizer runoff from farms beside the river is the primary cause. And most boaters don't even know the plant is endangered, so they don't avoid it. Plus, they normally can't see it because the rice stalks barely stick out of the water; therefore, boaters wind up hitting it while moving through the water. If you ask me, I'd say that Texas wild rice is doomed to extinction in the near future.

Sample Notes — LISTENING

Chances of survival for Texas wild rice are small

1   **efforts to conserve water = futile**
   –   population is growing + droughts reducing water level

2   **efforts to hunt nutria ineffective**
   –   breeds quickly = gives birth to 3 litters/year
   –   pesticides limited in effectiveness

3   **human actions = killing rice plants**
   –   chemical fertilizer runoff pollution hard to control
   –   boaters don't know to avoid plant + can't see it well

Both the reading passage and the lecture are about Texas wild rice and the efforts to keep it from going extinct. While the reading passage presents hope that it can be saved, the professor casts doubt on the arguments in the passage and believes the plant will go extinct soon.

The professor first mentions the water level of the San Marcos River, where Texas wild rice grows. He argues that the water level is being lowered by excessive use from the growing population and notes the negative effects of droughts. Those two points go against the argument made in the reading passage that people can use less water to keep the river's water level from dropping.

Next, the professor claims that hunting the nutria, which eats the rice plants, is useless. The author of the reading passage declares that enough nutria can be killed by hunters, trappers, and pesticides. But the professor believes that the nutria breeds too rapidly and that pesticides are not effective on it.

Last, the professor discusses human actions such as pollution and boating. Although the reading passage asserts that humans are learning to avoid damaging Texas wild rice, the professor says that chemicals from farms cause the most pollution. He also stresses that boaters cannot usually see the plants, so they hit the rice while they are in the water.

Chapter 02

A | Reading Passage p. 24

Outlining

Main Point: *Mary Celeste* = ship found drifting in water w/no crew → is mystery what happened

Argument 1: weather caused crew to abandon ship

- sails found in tatters
- water damage on ship → large waves may have hit

Argument 2: was potential for large explosion of industrial alcohol

- fumes could have leaked so crew feared explosion

Argument 3: crew mutinied

- blood found on deck + sword
- crew killed captain and escaped on lifeboat → kept quiet so weren't imprisoned

Paraphrasing Exercises

1 Damage from water in the cabins and water in the hold indicated that big waves had hit the ship.

2 The *Mary Celeste's* dangerous cargo of industrial alcohol

might have leaked some fumes.

3 The survivors did not want people to know what they did, so they would have remained quiet.

B | Listening Lecture p. 26

Listening Script

Now listen to part of a lecture on the topic you just read about.

M Professor: So, uh, those are the known facts about the *Mary Celeste*. Now comes the intriguing part . . . What caused her crew to abandon a seaworthy vessel? There are many hypotheses—some quite outlandish—but most historians have decided that three theories have the highest potential for being true. Even so, each of them has serious issues that make them doubtful. Let me explain . . .

It's almost certainly true that the ship was damaged by the elements, but the weather did not make the ship unseaworthy. In fact, the salvage crew that found the *Mary Celeste* sailed her all the way to Gibraltar, um, a considerable distance. Because the ship was in no danger of sinking, the captain surely wouldn't have ordered the crew to get into the small lifeboat.

Now, uh, the cargo, which was industrial alcohol, was known to leak fumes due to it being stored in wooden barrels back in the nineteenth century. Yet when British experts in Gibraltar examined the ship, they found no sign of explosive damage or fire. All the cargo hatches were secure, and, uh, except for a few barrels that had leaked a bit, the cargo was secure.

Foul play was long suspected but never proven conclusively. In fact, what were believed to be human bloodstains found on the ship were later shown by experts not to be human blood at all. No crew members had a previous history of violent crime. And while some people suspected the salvage crew might have killed everyone on the *Mary Celeste*, they were of high moral character and had never run afoul of the law before. The British Admiralty Court in Gibraltar eventually concluded there was insufficient evidence of murder and mayhem. So, uh, as you can see, we can't really support any of these theories.

Note-Taking

Main Point: are serious issues with all theories about *Mary Celeste*

Argument 1: weather didn't make ship unseaworthy

- salvage crew sailed ship to Gibraltar
- captain wouldn't have ordered crew into lifeboat

Argument 2: alcohol didn't explode

- no sign of explosion or fire + hatches were secure

Argument 3: no proof of foul play

- blood on deck wasn't human
- crew and salvage crew had no history of violence

Paraphrasing Exercises

1 The captain wouldn't have abandoned ship since it wasn't sinking.

2 Industrial alcohol often leaked fumes because of the barrels it was stored in in the 1800s.

3 Despite people's suspicions, the salvage crew was full of good people with no legal problems.

C Combining the Main Points p. 27

1 The professor acknowledges that the *Mary Celeste* was damaged by the weather, yet he points out that it was still seaworthy and was sailed to Gibraltar.

2 While the writer of the reading passage believes that the threat of an enormous explosion induced the crew to get on the ship's lifeboat and depart, the professor states that experts who studied the ship found little evidence of leakage and noted that there had been no explosions on the ship.

3 The professor remarks that the blood found on the ship's deck was not human blood and that investigators found no evidence of foul play. His declarations therefore challenge the one made in the reading passage that the crew mutinied, killed the captain, and then abandoned ship.

D Completing the Essay p. 28

Sample Essay

During his lecture, the professor discusses some of the widely accepted theories regarding what happened to the crew of the *Mary Celeste*. In doing so, he challenges the claims which are made in the reading passage.

The professor acknowledges that the *Mary Celeste* was damaged by the weather, yet he points out that it was still seaworthy and was sailed to Gibraltar. He therefore shows that the *Mary Celeste* was not in danger of sinking, so he proves that the argument that water damage and damage to the sails caused the crew to abandon the ship is inaccurate.

Another theory is that the crew feared the ship's cargo of industrial alcohol was leaking and could explode anytime. While the writer of the reading passage believes that the threat of an enormous explosion induced the crew to get on the ship's lifeboat and depart, the professor states that experts who studied the ship found little evidence of leakage and noted that there had been no explosions on the ship.

Finally, the professor mentions the theory that violence was involved. The professor remarks that the blood found on the ship's deck was not human blood and that investigators found

no evidence of foul play. His declarations therefore challenge the one made in the reading passage that the crew mutinied, killed the captain, and then abandoned ship.

---

iBT Practice Test p. 29

Sample Notes — READING

People skeptical that Phoenicians circumnavigated Africa

1 **ships weren't designed for open seas**
   - were made as coast huggers
   - sails couldn't tack into wind → would have been hard sailing north into wind

2 **Phoenicians were unfamiliar w/African coast**
   - didn't know currents, reefs, and winds
   - ships couldn't have survived → either turned back or sank

3 **weather was terrible**
   - Cape of Good Hope has strong winds and high waves → other places = calm winds for weeks
   - replica Phoenician ship sailed around Africa only due to modern technology

Listening Script

Now listen to part of a lecture on the topic you just read about.

W Professor: The first circumnavigation of Africa was accomplished in ancient times by Phoenician sailors in the year 600 B.C. How many ships and sailors took part is unknown. It is, however, known that Egyptian Pharaoh Necho the Second sponsored the voyage of the ships, which sailed south through the Indian Ocean and then moved counterclockwise around Africa. Despite evidence for the trip existing, many have regarded it as a myth. I, however, am positive that it took place.

First of all, modern skeptics point out that Phoenician ships were simply incapable of such a voyage due to their design. While it's true that their sails weren't designed to catch the wind, that wouldn't have been a problem when the wind wasn't blowing or when it was blowing toward them. You see, uh, the Phoenicians had slaves on their ships, and one of their many tasks was to row during periods of calm or contrary winds.

The Phoenicians were additionally, um, well versed at sailing into unknown waters. After all, they had ventured everywhere in the Mediterranean Sea, established colonies in various lands, and even sailed into the Atlantic Ocean and as far north as Britain. Sailing into the unknown didn't give them pause. They would have regarded the circumnavigation of Africa as a worthy challenge and would have surely completed the task.

When confronted by bad weather, the Phoenicians would have sheltered along the coast. Even if doing so required them to wait several months, they would have been able to get past the Cape of Good Hope. They also constructed sturdy ships capable of weathering major storms. A faithfully reproduced replica of a Phoenician vessel proved that a few years ago. Despite facing all kinds of dangerous winds and waves on its journey, it avoided sinking and successfully completed its voyage.

Sample Notes — LISTENING

Trip around Africa by Phoenicians took place

1 **getting past wind wouldn't have been a problem**
 – Phoenicians used slaves → could have rowed in calm weather or against contrary winds

2 **Phoenicians well versed at sailing in unknown waters**
 – had sailed around Mediterranean Sea and Atlantic Ocean up to Britain
 – sailing around Africa = challenge for them

3 **would have sheltered on coast in bad weather**
 – could have gotten past Cape of Good Hope
 – replica Phoenician ship faced dangerous winds and waves but completed voyage

Sample Essay

In her lecture, the professor discusses the possibility of the Phoenicians having completed a circumnavigation of Africa around 600 B.C. She discusses three problems raised in the reading passage and explains how the Phoenicians likely managed to overcome each one.

For starters, the professor acknowledges the point in the reading passage that Phoenician ships did not have sails which were designed to allow them to tack into the wind. However, she points out that the Phoenicians had slaves on board who would have been able to row in the face of contrary winds, so they could have sailed north up Africa's west coast.

Nor does she consider the fact that the Phoenicians did not know the waters around Africa a problem. She instead states that the Phoenicians enjoyed challenges and would have enjoyed trying to sail around Africa. To defend her argument, she mentions how the Phoenicians sailed to many other unknown lands.

The professor further notes that bad weather must have been an issue for the Phoenicians. However, while the author of the reading passage believes the Phoenicians would have had trouble with stormy weather, the professor disagrees, saying the ships could have sheltered during storms. She also cites the example of a replica Phoenician ship completing a journey around Africa in recent years as proof that the Phoenicians could have done it.

Chapter 03

A | Reading Passage
p. 32

Outlining

Main Point: cities should build high-speed express train systems

Argument 1: can use existing railway systems
 – don't need to build new roads or maintain them
 – less wear and tear on railways since less traffic

Argument 2: reduce traffic congestion
 – too many cars = traffic jams
 – no traffic jams for railroads → schedules controlled = know when will leave and arrive

Argument 3: reduce pollution
 – trains create less pollution than thousands of cars
 – idling cars = make more pollution

Paraphrasing Exercises

1 Trains can move more people then cars and buses, and the lower amounts of traffic mean that railways will wear down less than roads.

2 One train carries as many people as hundreds of cars, and those cars can cause big traffic jams.

3 A small number of trains will create less pollution than thousands of cars.

B | Listening Lecture
p. 34

Listening Script

Now listen to part of a lecture on the topic you just read about.

W Professor: All throughout the country, millions of people commute from suburbs to big cities every day. It's inevitable that there are going to be transportation problems. Now, uh, lately, some politicians have begun proposing building high-speed rail networks. But I've got to tell you that there are all kinds of problems with them.

For one thing, they're incredibly expensive. Don't be fooled by anyone who tries convincing you otherwise. Most railway tracks in the country are outdated, and so are the, um, the bridges and tunnels they use. They're in need of expensive upgrades, especially if the tracks are going to be used by even more trains. Express trains in particular require high-grade rails and safe routes because they travel at faster speeds than regular trains. Just building a single high-speed rail system in one area can require billions of dollars.

Now, uh, it's true that express trains would reduce road congestion in some places, but let's remember that most of the country isn't like the east coast. By that, um, I mean that along the eastern seaboard, millions of people reside in metropolitan areas and thus live close to train stations. But in the southern and western parts of the country, cities and suburbs tend to be more spread out, so public transportation isn't practical. People would have to drive their vehicles to stations, pay to park them, and then board trains. For those individuals, it would be easier and faster to drive.

Lastly, let's remember that trains—even electric ones—expend plenty of fuel and produce pollution, so they're not particularly ecofriendly. And when you consider that our existing rail systems don't allow trains to move quickly and suffer from plenty of delays, you'll realize that idling and slow-moving trains will expel even more pollution into the air.

Note-Taking

Main Point: are many problems with high-speed express trains

Argument 1: very expensive
- tracks, bridges, and tunnels need expensive upgrades
- express train need high-grade rails = cost billions of $ to make

Argument 2: many people don't live near train stations
- people in south and west → don't live near cities
- would have to drive to stations, park cars, and board trains = easier to drive

Argument 3: trains aren't ecofriendly
- use lots of fuel and produce pollution
- trains move slowly + delays = idling and slow-moving trains expel pollution

Paraphrasing Exercises

1 Express trains need high-grade rails and safe routes due to their high speeds.

2 In the south and west, cities are spread out, so public transportation is impractical.

3 Present-day rail systems have slow-moving trains and delays, which cause trains to expel lots of pollution.

C | Combining the Main Points p. 35

1 The professor believes that building train systems will cost billions of dollars, which is in opposition to the claim in the reading passage that it would be cheaper to build express train networks than to build and maintain roads.

2 The professor admits that some parts of the country could be helped by trains, but she also points out that the western and southern areas are spread out, so they are not ideal for commuters who want to take trains.

3 Although the reading passage claims that trains would

create less pollution than thousands of cars on the road, the professor disputes this notion. She says trains make plenty of pollution when they are both moving and idling, so they are not pollution free.

D | Completing the Essay p. 36

Sample Essay

The professor covers some disadvantages of building high-speed rail networks in her lecture. Her arguments against them cast doubt on some specific points supporting high-speed train systems that were made in the reading passage.

Both the reading passage and the professor discuss the costs of railway systems. The professor mentions that the American railway network is outdated and in need of upgrading. She believes that building train systems will cost billions of dollars, which is in opposition to the claim in the reading passage that it would be cheaper to build express train networks than to build and maintain roads.

The professor's second argument concerns the practicality of trains. She admits that some parts of the country could be helped by trains, but she also points out that the western and southern areas are spread out, so they are not ideal for commuters who want to take trains. Her argument thusly goes against the claim in the reading passage that trains would help numerous people commute each day.

Last, although the reading passage claims that trains would create less pollution than thousands of cars on the road, the professor disputes this notion. She says trains make plenty of pollution when they are both moving and idling, so they are not pollution free. Therefore there is no benefit to the environment by building train networks.

iBT Practice Test p. 37

Sample Notes — READING

Are benefits provided by zoning laws

1 **preserve property values**
- homeowners live in places w/few stores and office buildings
- if build factory, home loses value

2 **maintain integrity and safety of neighborhoods**
- prevent certain establishments from being built
- no nightclubs and bars near schools and housing areas
- preserve green lands in cities

3 **maintain historical integrity of communities**
- keep neighborhoods w/historical structures from being transformed
- don't let old buildings get ruined

Now listen to part of a lecture on the topic you just read about.

W Professor: While I understand the premise of zoning laws, they are interpreted too strictly at times. As a result, they tend to have deleterious effects on the neighborhoods they're theoretically looking after.

Arguably the biggest problem with zoning laws is that they infringe upon the individual rights of property owners. Sometimes people may want to sell their homes or land, but the zoning laws in their regions obstruct them. You remember how there were many local homeowners upset about the zoning laws here two months ago, right? What happened . . . ? Well, uh, an out-of-state company was planning to build a shopping mall, and it had agreed to purchase large plots of land. However, the city stepped in and, citing zoning laws, refused to let the mall be built there, so numerous property owners lost out on a great chance to get excellent value for their land.

Urban stagnation is something else that zoning laws contribute to. How . . . ? You see, uh, zoning laws prevent new businesses from moving into certain places, which causes some neighborhoods to remain the same for decades. Thus people have to travel far to find entertainment options since theaters, bars, and other similar places can't open in their neighborhoods. It's the same thing with parks. Yes, green areas are nice, but some cities have too many. And numerous parks sit on prime land that should be developed to improve the quality of cities and to keep them from stagnating.

A final issue concerns historical neighborhoods and buildings, which are traditionally protected by zoning laws. Sadly, these buildings often have structural problems or lack modern conveniences such as plumbing and wiring. They therefore inconvenience the people who live in them and can even endanger their lives since zoning laws may prohibit repair work or enhancements being done on the buildings.

Sample Notes — LISTENING

Zoning laws have bad effects on neighborhoods

1 infringe on rights of property owners
- want to sell land but can't because of zoning laws
- company wanted to open mall → people wanted to sell land → zoning laws prevented sale of land and opening of mall

2 create urban stagnation
- keep neighborhoods the same for decades
- people have to travel far for entertainment
- too many great areas → parks sitting on prime land

3 cause problems for historical neighborhoods and structures
- buildings have structural problems → zoning laws don't allow repair work
- buildings lack modern conveniences → zoning laws prohibit enhancements

Sample Essay

The author of the reading passage writes in support of zoning laws in cities. However, the professor disputes the arguments made in the reading passage and explains why she believes zoning laws are problematic.

The first problem with zoning laws that the professor covers concerns their effects on the rights of property owners. While the reading passage claims that zoning laws benefit homeowners by preventing businesses from setting up in residential areas, the professor says this prevents property owners from doing what they want with their land. She points out how zoning laws kept some local landowners from making lots of money recently.

The professor next argues against zoning laws on the basis that they cause stagnation in cities. She states that entertainment centers cannot be opened in certain places and that there are too many parks in some cities. According to her, both factors lead to urban stagnation. In that way, she challenges the argument in the reading passage that zoning laws keep neighborhoods safe and green.

The final argument against zoning laws that the professor makes is with regard to historical buildings and neighborhoods. While the reading passage praises zoning laws for keeping these buildings and places safe, the professor criticizes them because old buildings can be inconvenient to people on account of structural problems or the absence of modern conveniences.

Chapter 04

A | Reading Passage p. 40

Outlining

Main Point: should be legislation restricting importing and selling of invasive species

Argument 1: should regulate pet shops selling exotic animals
- many owners sell to careless individuals
- need legislation letting animals be seized or returned to countries of origin

Argument 2: provide funding to see how dangerous nonnative species are
- not sure how dangerous many species could be

– if species are potentially harmful, should ban them

Argument 3: ban importation of some species

– snakes and lizards → escape captivity easily
– best way to keep U.S. safe is to stop animals from entering country

Paraphrasing Exercises

1 Careless pet store owners sell exotic animals, which are hard to take care of, to anyone rather than those able to care for the animals.

2 If the studies show species could be harmful, they should be banned.

3 Preventing nonnative animals from entering the country is the best way to protect the United States.

B | Listening Lecture
p. 42

Listening Script

Now listen to part of a lecture on the topic you just read about.

W Professor: In recent weeks, some politicians have been discussing the need for legislation concerning exotic animals. These animals, which include snakes, alligators, tigers, lions, and iguanas, are said to be causing problems when they either escape or are released into the wild. While I agree that something needs to be done about this issue, I don't believe that the legislation being suggested will be effective. Here's why . . .

For starters, there's talk of seizing all the exotic animals owned by various pet stores. That poses a couple of problems. First, um, the government simply doesn't have the manpower or capability to raid thousands of pet stores across the country, to seize the animals, and then to keep them caged up. Second, the government would have to compensate the owners for their losses, and that could require millions, um, or even billions, of dollars in payments. The country can't afford that.

Next, I don't see how scientists can study the effects nonnative species might have if they were released into the wild without, uh, well, actually releasing some animals into the wild to find out what will happen. And do you know what . . . ? That's the last thing we want to see happen. Plus, it comes down to money again. It would be too expensive to conduct studies on every nonnative species of animals currently in the country.

Finally, well, I suppose the government could ban the importation of some species. But let's be honest . . . People are going to smuggle certain animals into the country someway. And those smuggled animals will be totally unregulated and unaccounted for. If you ask me, it would actually be safer to permit the animals into the country legally so that we can know exactly where they are and

who owns them. Banning them would cause more harm than good.

Note-Taking

Main Point: suggested legislation on exotic animals will not be effective

Argument 1: seizing animals at pet stores = problematic

– government doesn't have ability to raid stores and to seize animals
– lacks $ to compensate owners for losses

Argument 2: scientists can't learn about effects of animals

– would have to release animals into the wild to study them
– is too expensive

Argument 3: people would smuggle animals into country

– would be unregulated and unaccounted for
– safer to permit animals in country → can know where they are

Paraphrasing Exercises

1 The government is unable to red pet stores and then seize the animals in them.

2 There is no way to study the effects of nonnative species in the wild unless some of them are actually released into the wild.

3 Letting the animals into the country to know where they are would be safer.

C | Combining the Main Points
p. 43

1 First, the professor mentions that the government lacks the ability to conduct raids to seize the animals. Second, she points out that it would be too expensive to compensate the owners for the animals. In those ways, she goes against the argument in the reading passage that irresponsible pet store owners should have their exotic animals seized.

2 Although the reading passage argues that studies can be done, the professor states that invasive species would have to be released into the wild to see how they hurt the environment.

3 Unlike the reading passage, which argues in favor of banning the importing of various exotic animals, the professor thinks importing them should remain legal so that the animals can be monitored.

D | Completing the Essay
p. 44

Sample Essay

While lecturing, the professor discusses the issue of legislation concerning invasive species in the United States. She recognizes the animals as problems, but, unlike the author of the reading passage, she thinks the proposed legislation will be ineffective.

The professor doubts it would be prudent to seize exotic animals at pet stores around the country. First, she mentions that the government lacks the ability to conduct raids to seize the animals. Second, she points out that it would be too expensive to compensate the owners for the animals. In those ways, she goes against the argument in the reading passage that irresponsible pet store owners should have their exotic animals seized.

The professor also opposes conducting studies on which animals would cause harm to the environment. Although the reading passage argues that studies can be done, the professor states that invasive species would have to be released into the wild to see how they hurt the environment. She feels that would be counterproductive.

The final point the professor makes covers the banning of certain animals. She claims that if some animals were banned, people would start smuggling them into the country. So unlike the reading passage, which argues in favor of banning the importing of various exotic animals, she thinks importing them should remain legal so that the animals can be monitored.

iBT Practice Test   p. 45

Sample Notes ─ READING

Are benefits to reintroducing animals into places where they once lived but are now extinct

1 **restore equilibrium to region**
   - wolf once controlled deer population in Yellowstone
   - wolf disappeared → deer population rose
   - wolf was reintroduced in 1990s → deer overpopulation problem solved

2 **atone for wrongs done by humans**
   - beavers in Britain → went extinct due to human encroachment
   - trying to reintroduce them now

3 **prove viability of breeding animals in captivity**
   - raise animals on farms or ranches → then release into wild
   - has allowed numerous species to be reintroduced to former habitats

Listening Script

Now listen to part of a lecture on the topic you just read about.

M Professor: Reintroducing locally extinct species is a noble idea, yet it's flawed in practice. For every success story, there are countless failures. In fact, it's estimated that nearly seventy percent of all reintroduced species die in the wild soon after being released. What are some problems . . . ? Let me tell you . . .

Some people believe the reintroduced animals will remain in specific places, but that never happens. Instead, the animals go wherever they please. In Yellowstone National Park, wolves were released to help control the deer population. Well, uh, they succeeded spectacularly at that objective, but there's a problem. The wolves, you see, have begun roaming far from Yellowstone. They've encroached on human settlements and attacked farmers' animals. Naturally, the farmers are upset and are requesting that wolf hunting be legalized.

Another problem concerns those people trying to do good by reintroducing animals that humans caused to go extinct. In many instances, their efforts have become influenced by politics as those in power use the animals to show their commitment to environmental issues. Unfortunately, the reality of the situation is often, uh, ignored. The people trying to reintroduce beavers to Britain have overlooked the fact that there are few places in that country where beavers can actually live because Britain simply has too many people. As a result, their efforts are doomed to fail.

Here's another problem . . . Some people raise animals in captivity and then release them into the wild . . . These animals simply can't cope in the wild. One British study tracked forty-five animals—all carnivorous mammals belonging to seventeen different species—that were released in this manner. Only thirty percent survived over the long term. The others were killed by hunters, run over by cars, or starved to death since they didn't know how to hunt for the food they needed.

Sample Notes ─ LISTENING

Are problems with reintroducing species to former habitats

1 **animals don't stay in specific places**
   - wolves in Yellowstone roam far from park → attack farmers' animals
   - farmers want to hunt wolves

2 **efforts influenced by politics**
   - people want to show commitment to environment → ignore reality
   - Britain has too many people → reintroduction of beavers will fail

3 **animals raised in captivity can't cope in wild**
   - study on 17 species → 30% survived in long term
   - others killed by humans or starved since didn't know how to hunt

Sample Essay

The professor and the author of the reading passage both cover the issue of reintroducing species to lands where they once lived. The reading passage argues in favor of doing so, yet the professor points out several problems which can occur.

The first point the professor lectures on is wolves in Yellowstone National Park. Both the professor and the reading passage agree that the wolves solved the deer overpopulation issue. However, the professor claims that the practice was not a success because the wolves are leaving the park area and killing livestock, resulting in farmers wanting to hunt them.

The professor next argues against reintroducing animals to areas where they were wiped out due to human actions. He brings up the effort to reintroduce beavers to Britain. The reading passage claims that beavers can live there successfully, but the professor says that Britain has too many people, so the plan will fail.

Last of all, the professor dislikes the practice of raising animals in captivity and then releasing them into the wild. While the reading passage states that lots of animals have been successfully reintroduced through this method, the professor points out that more of them die. Citing a study in Britain, he remarks that only thirty percent of the animals survive while the others are killed by humans or starve to death.

Chapter 05

A | Reading Passage p. 48

Outlining

Main Point: are some theories on how flat ceramic disks were used

Argument 1: used for cooking
- were flat and could withstand heat → used as frying pans
- placed on tripods or balanced on rocks → food cooked on them

Argument 2: were musical instruments
- used as drums
- could beat with hands or with sticks

Argument 3: used as mirrors
- had reflective surfaces
- would have been popular in societies w/no metallurgy or glassware

Paraphrasing Exercises

1 Since they were flat and could withstand heat, the disks could have been used as frying pans.

2 People could have held the disks or balanced them on stands and then beat them to make music.

3 The images would have been poor but would have let people see themselves.

B | Listening Lecture p. 50

Listening Script

Now listen to part of a lecture on the topic you just read about.

M Professor: Take a look at this object on the screen . . . It's a flat ceramic disk. Disks like this one have been found at different dig sites in various places around the world, but, um, guess what . . . We're not really sure what they were used for. Of course, uh, archaeologists have come up with some theories regarding their purposes. But if you ask me, each of the three leading theories has some problems. Why don't I tell you about them now . . . ?

There are some who believe that these flat disks were used for cooking. You know, uh, they were used like frying pans. But look at the disk currently on screen . . . Do you see any scorch marks, discoloration from fire, or food residue on it . . . ? I don't. And no disks found have any of those marks on them, so, uh, since there's no physical evidence, I think we can discount this theory.

Now, uh, what would you say if I told you that the flat ceramic disks were used as musical instruments, uh, such as drums . . . ? Yeah, I can see some of you grinning. That's a rather farfetched theory, isn't it . . . ? Ceramics are a poor means of transmitting musical tones, which is in evidence today by the lack of musical instruments made of ceramics. Hollowed-out wood or cured animal hides stretched over wooden frames were the preferred means of making drums in ancient times, not ceramics.

A third prominent theory—that ceramic disks were once mirrors—is laughable for the simple reason that ceramics don't have highly reflective surfaces. Sure, they can reflect images, but not well enough to serve as mirrors. And consider that mirrors from ancient times were almost always decorated since mirrors were personal items. Well, uh, the ceramic disks unearthed thus far have no decorations at all.

Note-Taking

Main Point: are problems w/3 leading theories on flat ceramic disks

Argument 1: weren't used for cooking
- lack scorch marks, discoloration from fire, or food residue
- no physical evidence were used to cook with

Argument 2: weren't musical instruments
- ceramics transmit musical tones poorly
- used wood or animal hides to make instruments in past

Argument 3: weren't mirrors
- lack highly reflective surfaces
- mirrors were personal items w/decorations but disks lack decorations

1 Since there are no marks on the ceramic disks, the theory should be disregarded.

2 Ceramics don't transmit sound well, so there aren't modern musical instruments made of them.

3 The theory that the disks were mirrors is wrong because ceramics don't have highly reflective surfaces.

C | Combining the Main Points p. 51

1 The professor points out the absence of scorch marks and food residue on the disks, so this disproves the notion in the reading passage that the ceramic disks were placed over fire and then used to cook food on.

2 In stating that ceramics are poor materials for musical instruments and that wood and animal skins were favored as musical instruments, the professor proves that the idea that ceramic disks were beaten like drums is inaccurate.

3 While both the professor and the reading passage admit that the disks have reflective surfaces, the professor says that the reflections are too poor to have been used as mirrors.

D | Completing the Essay p. 52

Sample Essay

The professor talks to the students about some theories regarding the uses of flat ceramic disks unearthed at archaeological dig sites. In the process of his lecture, the professor discusses some problems with the main theories on how the disks were utilized.

The first theory mentioned is that the disks were used as cooking appliances. The professor, however, disregards this theory. He points out the absence of scorch marks and food residue on the disks, so this disproves the notion in the reading passage that the ceramic disks were placed over fire and then used to cook food on.

The second theory claims that the disks were ancient musical instruments. The professor doubts this for a couple of reasons. In stating that ceramics are poor materials for musical instruments and that wood and animal skins were favored as musical instruments, the professor proves that the idea that ceramic disks were beaten like drums is inaccurate.

The third theory is the belief that the disks were mirrors. But the professor disregards this theory as well. While both the professor and the reading passage admit that the disks have reflective surfaces, the professor says that the reflections are too poor to have been used as mirrors. He adds that the disks have no decorations, which most ancient mirrors had.

Sample Notes — READING

Sphinx was built before the time of Pharaoh Khafre

1 **weathering of Sphinx**
   - was not caused by wind and sand but by water
   - hasn't rained much since Khafre's time but rained a lot in Egypt prior to then

2 **no inscriptions saying Khafre built it**
   - Egyptians always left inscriptions about builders
   - if Khafre built it, he would have left written proof

3 **Sphinx's original face wasn't Khafre's**
   - head was worked on in past
   - existed before Khafre became pharaoh → changed face to resemble his own

Listening Script

Now listen to part of a lecture on the topic you just read about.

M Professor: One of the most controversial matters in Egyptology concerns the age of the Sphinx. Some academics believe it was made more than, uh, 5,000 years ago. However, traditionally, the Pharaoh Khafre is credited with having built it around 2550 B.C., and that's when I feel the Sphinx was made.

Some Egyptologists think the weathering patterns on the Sphinx are indicative of rain rather than wind and sand. Since Egypt has been mostly arid desert since Khafre's time, obviously, they argue, the Sphinx was built before then and was later rained on. That's just not true though. Why not . . . ? Well, the Sphinx is made of limestone, which is brittle. And the desert there has a high salt content. Even a tiny bit of moisture can draw salt into cracks in limestone. Then, the salt expands and causes some pieces of limestone to break off. This type of erosion looks like rain caused it, and that's precisely what happened to the Sphinx over time.

Now, uh, some say there are no inscriptions around the Sphinx indicating Khafre built it. Sure, but let's keep in mind that it was just one of many structures built in connection with Khafre's Pyramid. Inscriptions mentioning Khafre as well as statues of the pharaoh have been found there, so it's verified that he built the pyramid and other structures. Plus, most of the limestone dug out around the Sphinx was used to build the other structures, which is another connection.

Finally, uh, the assertion that the Sphinx's face isn't that of Khafre is wrong. The Sphinx once had a braided beard, just like Khafre has in a statue of him that has survived to this day, but the beard eroded and fell off. Let me assure you that the face of the Sphinx definitely used to resemble

Khafre's.

Sphinx was made around 2550 B.C.

1 **weathering patterns caused by limestone erosion**
  – looks like rain caused it
  – but was caused by salt making cracks in limestone

2 **are inscriptions about Khafre's Pyramid**
  – Sphinx belongs to Khafre's Pyramid complex
  – inscriptions mention he built all the structures

3 **Sphinx once looked like Khafre's face**
  – had brained beard → eroded and fell off
  – resembled face of Khafre as seen on statue of him

Sample Essay

The professor and the author of the reading passage discuss the Sphinx's age. While the professor believes it was made around 2550 B.C., the author of the reading passage thinks the Sphinx was built earlier.

The first point the professor brings up concerns erosion. Unlike the author of the reading passage, he does not believe the Sphinx endured water erosion. Instead, he claims that salt in the desert got into cracks in the limestone the Sphinx is made of and caused erosion that appears to be made by water but is not. Hence the professor doubts the claim in the reading passage that the Sphinx was built before Pharaoh Khafre's reign when it used to rain heavily in Egypt.

The second point the professor makes concerns the lack of inscriptions regarding who made the Sphinx. The reading passage argues that the absence of inscriptions proves Khafre did not make the Sphinx. But the professor mentions that there were many inscriptions stating that Khafre had the structures in Khafre's Pyramid built, which proves he made the Sphinx.

The third point is about the face of the Sphinx. Although the reading passage declares that the Sphinx's face was changed during the time of Khafre, the professor disagrees and declares that the Sphinx once had a beard like Khafre, but it eroded and fell off.

Chapter 06

A | Reading Passage   p. 56

Outlining

Main Point: are several ways for companies to grow more and to be more successful

Argument 1: tweak existing products
– can create similar but new products → household cleaning products
– existing consumers buy more + get new consumers

Argument 2: sell ancillary products
– are related to main product
– car companies → sell vehicle accessories
– computer companies → sell add-ons

Argument 3: branch out from core products to sell unrelated ones
– can elevate sales
– Sony → has sold many different types of products → innovates

Paraphrasing Exercises

1 Current customers will buy the products since they think they are better, and new customers will buy them, too.

2 Computer companies sell add-ons to improve the quality of their computers.

3 Some companies start selling products other than their core ones.

B | Listening Lecture   p. 58

Listening Script

Now listen to part of a lecture on the topic you just read about.

M Professor: Companies are always looking for ways to increase their revenues and profits. Most people just say that companies need to innovate to come up with new products. But, well, it isn't as easy at that. . .

Marketing experts often advise companies to change their products a bit to make them newer and better. But guess what . . . Lots of customers don't like change but instead prefer the original products. I remember back in the 1980s when Coca-Cola changed the formula for Coke. New Coke was an absolute failure. People hated the way it tasted, and sales dropped dramatically. It didn't take long for the company to recognize the mistake it had made and to start selling Coke with the original recipe again.

Now, uh, another thing companies do is try to convince their customers to purchase add-ons. Sure, this can increase sales, but it really irritates customers, especially when salespeople employ aggressive tactics. Just the other day, my mobile phone broke, so I visited a store to purchase a new one. All I wanted was a phone, but the salesperson kept trying to convince me to buy accessories, uh, such as a recharger and a case, for it. By the time I left, I was so mad that I had decided never to return to that store again.

Yet another idea that often ends in failure is when companies enter entirely new markets. You might see an appliance maker start selling clothes or a computer manufacturer enter the automobile market. Doing that is highly risky. Why . . . ? Well, the companies have to spend vast fortunes on research and development, production, and marketing, but people don't associate them with the new products, so customers don't purchase them. To be honest, entering a new market is a great way for a company to bankrupt itself.

Note-Taking

Main Point: isn't easy for companies to innovate

Argument 1: customers often don't like change
- Coca-Cola changed to New Coke in 1980s → failed
- people hated taste → sales dropped → company began selling original Coke

Argument 2: salespeople can aggravate customers
- keep asking to buy add-ons
- visited store to buy phone → salesperson was annoying → decided never to go back to store again

Argument 3: can fail when enter new markets
- highly risky → must spend lots of $ on R&D, production, and marketing
- customers don't buy → companies go bankrupt

Paraphrasing Exercises

1 The company quickly admitted its mistakes and began selling original Coke.

2 I got so upset that I decided never to visit that store again.

3 Companies spend lots of money on the new products, but people don't buy them since they don't associate the companies with them.

C | Combining the Main Points

p. 59

1 By noting that this change failed and that the company started making Coke with the original formula again, the professor casts doubt on the notion in the reading passage that using "new and improved" formulas can improve a company's sales.

2 The author of the reading passage claims that some companies are very effective at getting customers to buy extra items, but the professor argues that the salespeople can be so bothersome that customers may stop visiting

their stores.

3 The author of the reading passage cites Sony as an example of a company that has successfully done this. However, the professor points out that entering new markets is expensive and frequently results in companies going bankrupt.

D | Completing the Essay

p. 60

Sample Essay

Both the lecture and the reading passage focus on methods by companies to improve their profits. While the author of the reading passage supports some of the ways companies try to become more successful, the professor explains how these methods can fail.

The professor first examines what can happen when companies alter their original products and create new ones. He talks about how Coca-Cola changed the formula for Coke in the 1980s. By noting that this change failed and that the company started making Coke with the original formula again, he casts doubt on the notion in the reading passage that using "new and improved" formulas can improve a company's sales.

The professor also discusses how companies attempt to get customers to purchase add-ons to their products. The author of the reading passage claims that some companies are very effective at getting customers to buy extra items, but the professor argues that the salespeople can be so bothersome that customers may stop visiting their stores.

Finally, both the professor and the reading passage mention that some companies sell items unrelated to their core products. The author of the reading passage cites Sony as an example of a company that has successfully done this. However, the professor points out that entering new markets is expensive and frequently results in companies going bankrupt.

iBT Practice Test

p. 61

Sample Notes — READING

Online advertising > print advertising

1 **reach more people than printed ads**
- printed ads have limited print runs
- people around world can see online ads

2 **online ads are cheaper**
- prices determined by number of clicks → can limit clicks to set budget
- pay set prices for printed ads → can be tens of thousands of dollars or more

3 **better for specialized markets**

- company selling sporting equipment → buys ads on sports news websites
- readers more likely to purchase than regular newspaper readers

Now listen to part of a lecture on the topic you just read about.

W Professor: These days, many companies prefer advertising online instead of in newspapers and magazines. But I think that's a big mistake because there are still a number of advantages to printed advertisements.

Supporters of online ads assert that the advertisements reach many more people than printed advertisements, but I'm not so sure that's true. For one thing, how many of you ever click on online ads . . . ? Yeah, not too many. I never do. In fact, like many people, I use ad-blocking software on my computer to avoid seeing any ads. As for printed ads, let's remember that many people, such as the elderly, don't use computers. And they often have lots of money, so they have a great deal of purchasing power.

Now, uh, it's true that online ads are cheaper than printed ads, but that doesn't make them more effective. Consider that many firms limit the number of people who can view their online ads on a monthly basis. Sure, that saves money, but it decreases how many people can look at their ads. With a printed ad, a company pays a flat fee, and there's no limit to the number of eyeballs that can view it. And consider that a newspaper or magazine may be read by multiple people, especially in households, so companies are getting access to more people without having to pay more money.

Finally, printed ads are actually ideal for specialized markets, especially local ones. Do you know that bakery right off campus? It constantly advertises in the local paper. It doesn't need to advertise online. What's the point of putting ads online for people in other countries to read when it doesn't deliver to them? Instead, it advertises only to local customers, so it effectively utilizes its advertising budget.

Sample Notes — LISTENING

Printed ads have many advantages

1 **few people click on online ads**
   - use ad-blocking software
   - elderly and others don't use computers → have lots of $

2 **online ads aren't more effective than printed ads**
   - limit number of clicks = limit number of people seeing ads
   - no limit to number of people who read newspapers or magazines

3 **printed ads ideal for specialized markets**

- local bakery → advertises in local paper
- doesn't need online ads because doesn't deliver to other countries

Sample Essay

In her lecture, the professor discusses the benefits printed ads have over online ads. By doing so, she challenges the arguments made in the reading passage, which promotes online ads.

The professor is skeptical of the claim in the reading passage that more people see online advertisements than printed ones. She points out that many people never click on online ads, and she adds that many individuals, including herself, use ad-blocking software, so she believes it is not necessarily true that online ads are viewed more.

The next point she considers is the prices of the ads. While the professor acknowledges that printed ads are more expensive than online ones, she states that some companies lower costs by reducing the number of customers that can click on their ads, thereby reducing their effectiveness. She then states that the prices of printed ads do not rise if more people see them.

Finally, the professor remarks that many companies have no need to advertise online. She uses an example of a local bakery by stating that it does not deliver to distant places, so having online ads is pointless for it. Instead, it purchases local advertising. By bringing up that example, she opposes the statement in the reading passage that many companies are better off advertising offline than in specialized markets.

Chapter 07

A | Reading Passage   p. 64

Outlining

Main Point: are efforts to improve environment of Chesapeake Bay

Argument 1: overfishing is big problem
- fishermen caught too many crabs → caught many spawning females
- quotas limiting number of crabs caught → blue crab population increasing

Argument 2: bay polluted by fertilizer runoff
- chemicals in fertilizer get into bay → create algae blooms
- strict controls on chemical usage and runoff = pollutants in bay reduced

Argument 3: try to increase oyster population
- oysters can extract pollutants from water
- plan to introduce Asian oysters → can help clean up bay

1 Quotas on the number of crabs being caught are letting the blue crab population in the bay recover.

2 Controls on chemical usage and runoff since 2009 have reduced pollutants in the bay.

3 Asian oysters are adept since they have many advantages over local oysters.

B | Listening Lecture   p. 66

Listening Script

Now listen to part of a lecture on the topic you just read about.

W Professor: I remember how dirty Chesapeake Bay used to be a few decades ago, so I'm rather pleased to see people interested in cleaning up the area. But I must say that the ongoing solutions and proposed ones have, well, they have significant problems which people need to be made aware of.

For one thing, establishing quotas on the number of fish that can be caught will definitely help fish stocks increase, yet it will simultaneously hurt local fishermen. Remember that there are numerous small communities whose residents depend on fishing for their livelihoods, so quotas will reduce their ability to make a living. And note that fishermen argue that some of these quotas have been enacted due to erroneous counts by government workers. They contend that the government is undercounting the number of fish in the bay, so there really isn't a need for quotas.

Now, uh, I applaud the efforts to control agricultural runoff because algae blooms are really harmful. However . . . they're not the only source of pollution in the bay. What else is there . . . ? Well, sewage from towns and cities and runoff from forests sprayed with insecticides both wind up in the bay. Combined, they cause a significant amount of harm to the bay, but politicians are ignoring these issues, so they will continue to be problems in the future.

Oh, here's another one . . . Some conservationists are hoping to introduce Asian oysters into the bay to filter out pollutants. What an awful idea. Asian oysters are a nonnative species that would likely grow out of control and replace the native oysters. They could additionally cause all sorts of problems, especially if they migrate to other regions along the eastern seaboard. We simply shouldn't be introducing invasive species into the bay. That would be disastrous.

Note-Taking

Main Point: ongoing solutions and proposed ones have problems

Argument 1: quotas hurt fishermen

– communities w/fishermen need to catch fish for livelihoods
– fishermen say government is undercounting fish in bay → no need for quotas

Argument 2: many sources of pollution in bay

– sewage + runoff w/insecticides = getting into bay
– politicians are ignoring so will continue being problems

Argument 3: mistake to introduce Asian oysters

– nonnative species → could grow out of control and replace native oysters
– may migrate elsewhere in region = disastrous

Paraphrasing Exercises

1 The residents of small communities will be hurt by quotas since they are filled with fishermen.

2 They are harming the bay, but politicians are ignoring them, so they will continue to be harmful.

3 They could cause many other problems if they migrate to the eastern seaboard.

C | Combining the Main Points   p. 67

1 Although the professor agrees with the reading passage that the quotas will result in an increase in the amount of marine life in the bay, she points out a negative aspect of the quotas. They are directly harming the fishermen whose livelihoods depend upon the fish they catch in Chesapeake Bay.

2 Yet she states that the issue of sewage and insecticides getting into the bay is not being handled, so unlike the author of the reading passage, she thinks the runoff issue is not being treated sufficiently.

3 The author of the reading passage supports importing the oysters, but the professor speaks strongly against it. She believes that introducing an invasive species to the bay could cause many future problems.

D | Completing the Essay   p. 68

Sample Essay

The professor's lecture provides a pessimistic view of the ongoing efforts to solve the problems in Chesapeake Bay. She has a much different opinion than the author of the reading passage, who is more optimistic about the recovery efforts.

To begin with, the professor comments on the fishing quotas being enacted in Chesapeake Bay. Although the professor agrees with the reading passage that the quotas will result in an increase in the amount of marine life in the bay, she points out a negative aspect of the quotas. They are directly harming the fishermen whose livelihoods depend upon the fish they catch in Chesapeake Bay.

A second point the professor discusses is runoff in the bay. Like the author of the reading passage, she approves of the fact that agricultural runoff causing algae blooms is being controlled. Yet she states that the issue of sewage and insecticides getting into the bay is not being handled, so unlike the author of the reading passage, she thinks the runoff issue is not being treated sufficiently.

The third point mentioned is the introduction of Asian oysters in the bay to remove pollutants from the water. The author of the reading passage supports importing the oysters, but the professor speaks strongly against it. She believes that introducing an invasive species to the bay could cause many future problems.

iBT Practice Test

Sample Notes — READING

Ways to get rid of lionfish being devised

1 **grouper hunts lionfish**
   - propose quotas on grouper fishing
   - increase grouper population → can hunt more lionfish

2 **encourage people to kill lionfish**
   - ask fishermen and divers with spear guns to kill them
   - may not kill many but can reduce their numbers

3 **promote consumption of lionfish**
   - tastes delicious → educated people on taste
   - increase demand for lionfish = more fishermen catch them

Listening Script

Now listen to part of a lecture on the topic you just read about.

W Professor: In the late 1990s, the lionfish population in the Atlantic Ocean and Caribbean Sea began increasing. Today, the fish is a serious problem as it consumes numerous commercial species of fish and is endangering many coral reefs as well. Of course, people are coming up with ways to solve the lionfish problem, but, if you ask me, the lionfish population is simply too large and widespread to be controlled.

Some people are hoping to increase the grouper population by protecting the fish since groupers hunt lionfish. However, lionfish have an effective tactic against groupers. They, uh, they eat juvenile groupers. Basically, um, lionfish kill groupers before the fish become big enough to hunt them. In doing so, lionfish are ensuring their own survival. Oh, and many people in the Caribbean don't want to protect the grouper since they make their living catching it.

I've heard that both fishermen and divers are being encouraged to catch and kill lionfish. Well, look at this picture before you decide to hunt them . . . Notice the protruding spines on the lionfish. Nasty, huh? Those spines, by the way, produce a venom that's painful to humans and is sometimes even fatal. So you need to be careful around lionfish if you're trying to catch them, and that makes most people just avoid them in general.

Some people are promoting the eating of lionfish. Sure, they taste great, but those spines and venom are two reasons lionfish isn't on many restaurant menus. For one, preparing the fish requires special skills to prevent accidental poisoning. Next, many people are afraid of eating animals with poison in their bodies no matter how well the meat is prepared and cooked. So I doubt that lionfish is going to become popular in most places.

Sample Notes — LISTENING

Can't control lionfish population

1 **problem w/using groupers**
   - lionfish eat juvenile groupers → eat them before grow bigger
   - many in Caribbean make living catching grouper so don't want it protected

2 **lionfish is dangerous**
   - has spines with venom → can be fatal to humans
   - have to be careful around lionfish

3 **many don't want to eat lionfish**
   - spines and venom scare people
   - must prepare fish properly or can be poisoned

Sample Essay

The focus of the lecture and the reading passage is the lionfish, a nuisance fish which is increasing in number in the Caribbean Sea and parts of the Atlantic Ocean. Whereas the writer of the reading passage believes the lionfish population can be controlled, the professor has her doubts.

She starts by talking about efforts to increase the grouper population since groupers hunt and kill lionfish. The writer of the reading passage remarks that establishing quotas on grouper fishing will increase the grouper population, but the professor notes that lionfish hunt juvenile groupers, which are unable to hunt lionfish. She also says that many Caribbean fishermen catch groupers, so she does not believe the grouper population will increase much.

While the writer of the reading passage declares that fishermen and divers can be convinced to catch and kill lionfish, the professor is skeptical of this claim. She says the spines of lionfish have dangerous venom, so catching lionfish is something few people want to do.

The last argument concerns people eating lionfish. The professor says that people will not eat much lionfish since preparing it is hard and few people want to eat something potentially fatal. Those two points counter the argument in the reading passage that spreading the word about the delicious taste of lionfish will convince more people to eat it.

Chapter 08

A | Reading Passage

Outlining

Main Point: are some hypotheses on why birds do anting

Argument 1: for molting
- do anting same time when molt
- birds' skin irritated by molting → ant secretions soothe skin

Argument 2: to remove parasites
- ants secrete formic acid → can kill lice and mites on birds
- birds take baths in acid to remove parasites = cleans bodies

Argument 3: to prepare ants to be eaten
- ants secrete defensive liquids → could harm birds if eat ants
- ants deplete secretions → birds can eat ants

Paraphrasing Exercises

1 Ornithologists like the theory since birds molt and do anting at the same time of year.

2 Scientists think birds bathe in formic acid to cleanse their bodies of parasites.

3 By touching the ants, the birds cause the ants to secrete defensive liquids.

B | Listening Lecture

Listening Script

Now listen to part of a lecture on the topic you just read about.

M Professor: So, uh, that's a description of anting. It sounds pretty strange, doesn't it . . . ? And the thing is that we've known about anting for a long time, yet we don't know for sure why birds do it. Oh, yeah, there are some theories, but there are holes in each of them.

For instance, it's true that birds often do anting at the same time that they molt, so I suppose there's a possibility that the two actions are related. But here's the thing: We don't really know if birds get irritated skin from molting and if the acidic liquids produced by the ants help relieve any, um, any itching sensations. It could be a complete coincidence that birds do both activities around the same time.

Another school of thought claims that birds use anting

to induce the release of formic acid by ants to kill various parasites on the birds' skin. Well, um, it's true that formic acid can kill many parasites, but attempts at getting birds to engage in anting in laboratories have failed to reach any conclusions. In addition, you should be aware that nearly all birds have parasites on their skin and feathers, but not all birds engage in anting. Only some species do.

A relatively new theory claims that anting induces ants to secrete acidic defensive liquids which could harm birds. Then, after the liquids have been depleted from the ants' bodies, the ants are more edible to the birds. This theory has the added benefit of having been replicated once in a lab. But . . . that was in a controlled environment, so the results are inconclusive. In addition, birds have been observed rubbing millipedes, beetles, and even flowers on their feathers, but the birds weren't seen eating those things afterward.

Note-Taking

Main Point: all theories on anting have holes

Argument 1: don't know if molting irritates birds' skin
- liquids secreted by ants might not help
- could be coincidence that molt and do anting at same time

Argument 2: lab tests on anting are inconclusive
- not sure if do it to release formic acid
- most birds have parasites, but not all birds do anting

Argument 3: lab tests were in controlled environment
- therefore tests are inconclusive
- birds rub other substances on bodies → didn't eat them later

Paraphrasing Exercises

1 We are not sure if molting irritates the skin of birds or if ant secretions relieve any feelings of itchiness.

2 While formic acid kills parasites, lab tests on birds were inconclusive.

3 Birds have been seen rubbing various substances on their bodies yet did not eat them later.

C | Combining the Main Points

1 The author of the reading passage supports this theory, but the professor says it could be coincidental that birds molt and do anting at the same time.

2 The professor admits that formic acid eliminates parasites, but he comments that laboratory tests on anting were inconclusive while also noting that not all birds do anting even though most of them have parasites.

3 According to the reading passage, the secretions are only harmful if the ants are eaten. While the professor acknowledges that this happened in a laboratory

experiment, he also remarks that birds rub other insects and flowers on their bodies but do not eat them.

D | Completing the Essay

Sample Essay

The professor's lecture is about anting, an activity in which birds rub ants on their bodies or let ants crawl on them. The author of the reading passage proposes three theories regarding why birds do anting, but the professor finds fault with each one.

The first theory the professor mentions is that birds do anting to get ants to secrete substances that can make their skin feel less irritated after they molt. The author of the reading passage supports this theory, but the professor says it could be coincidental that birds molt and do anting at the same time.

Another hypothesis proposed in the reading passage is that anting causes ants to release formic acid, which kills parasites on birds' bodies. The professor admits that formic acid eliminates parasites, but he comments that laboratory tests on anting were inconclusive while also noting that not all birds do anting even though most of them have parasites.

A final theory the professor disregards is that birds induce ants to release defensive secretions by engaging in anting. According to the reading passage, the secretions are only harmful if the ants are eaten. While the professor acknowledges that this happened in a laboratory experiment, he also remarks that birds rub other insects and flowers on their bodies but do not eat them.

iBT Practice Test

Sample Notes — READING

Three reasons mountain yellow-legged frog population has declined

1 **trout**
   - were introduced into frogs' ecosystem → upset balance
   - trout feed on tadpoles and juveniles
   - frogs lacked instinct to flee

2 **pesticides**
   - enter water system → contaminate water
   - kill many frogs

3 **deadly fungus**
   - attacks adult frogs → destroys keratin in bodies
   - weakens frogs → can die up to two weeks after getting infected

Listening Script

Now listen to part of a lecture on the topic you just read about.

W Professor: Attempts to add the mountain yellow-legged frog to the endangered species list finally ended in success in 2013, but it may be too late for us to prevent the frog from going extinct. One reason is that we're not quite sure what has caused its numbers to decline so precipitously. Without that knowledge, it'll be hard to determine how to go about saving the animal.

There are many who blame the trout living in the waterways of the Sierra Nevada Mountains for the decline of the frog population. While it's true that the trout catch and eat lots of frogs, consider this fact . . . Trout were introduced to that area more than 100 years ago, but it wasn't until around, oh, forty years ago that the frog population entered into decline. So for more than sixty years, the trout and frogs lived together in a state of equilibrium.

Pesticides, which enter water systems along with rain and snow runoff, are similarly blamed for killing the frogs. However, the strongest concentrations of pesticides are always at the lower levels of the mountains since, uh, water flows downhill. But . . . frogs are dying at the upper, middle, and lower levels of the mountains, so I don't believe pesticides are solely to blame either.

Now, um, in recent decades, a deadly fungus has been killing lots of species of frogs in the region. The mountain yellow-legged frog has a defense against the fungus though. What defense . . . ? Well, it can cover its skin in secretions which protect it from the fungus. Of course, uh, the fungus still manages to kill some frogs, but most of the frogs are able to protect themselves from it. So, um, if you ask me, there must be something else we haven't discovered yet that's killing so many frogs.

Sample Notes — LISTENING

Not sure why frog population is declining

1 **trout may not be responsible**
   - were introduced 100+ years ago
   - frogs only started declining 40 years ago

2 **pesticides may not be responsible**
   - strongest pesticide concentrations at lowest levels
   - but frogs dying at all levels of mountains

3 **frog has protection from fungus**
   - can cover self with skin secretions
   - some frogs die, but many can protect selves

Sample Essay

The topic of the lecture and the reading passage is the numerous deaths of the mountain yellow-legged frog, which have caused it to be placed on the endangered species list. In the reading passage, three possible causes for the deaths of the frog are proposed, but the professor disregards each hypothesis.

The professor agrees with the author of the reading passage that trout, which are a nonnative species in the Sierra Nevada Mountains, eat lots of frogs. However, she tells her students that the trout and frogs have lived together for a century but the frog population only began declining forty years ago. She therefore disagrees with the reading passage that the trout upset the balance of the ecosystem in which the frogs reside.

Next, the professor again agrees that pesticides which get into the water kill lots of frogs. But she mentions that frogs are dying everywhere on the mountains, not just in their lower levels, which have the highest concentrations of pesticides.

Lastly, the professor discusses a fungus which is killing many frogs. Although she agrees that some frogs are killed by the fungus, she remarks that they have a defense against it since they can cover their skin in a secretion which keeps them safe from the fungus. So she believes something else must be causing the frogs to die.

Chapter 09

A | Reading Passage

Outlining

Main Point: people want to eliminate cheatgrass

Argument 1: physically destroy it
- cut w/mowers, till, or pull up by roots
- can use fires to kill

Argument 2: letting livestock graze on it
- when sprouts, is high in protein → beneficial to animals
- best time to graze is when first comes up

Argument 3: using chemicals
- spray herbicides from backpacks or crop dusters
- best times to kill are in fall and spring

Paraphrasing Exercises

1 People can kill cheatgrass by cutting it, tilling it, or pulling it up from the ground.

2 New cheatgrass is rich in protein and can benefit the livestock that eats it.

3 People can spray herbicides in small fields or use crop dusters for big infestations.

B | Listening Lecture

Listening Script

Now listen to part of a lecture on the topic you just read about.

W Professor: This is a picture of cheatgrass . . . It's an invasive weed that's becoming a tremendous problem in many parts of the United States and Canada. It's dominating other grasses and is also a fire hazard since mature plants easily catch fire and burn quickly. People everywhere are trying to eliminate cheatgrass, and, while they've encountered some success, there are problems with the methods being employed.

Some people mow cheatgrass or till it, and that works on small areas, but it's not practical for areas with lots of cheatgrass. In addition, those two methods don't kill the plant since it grows back. Thus people have to keep mowing or tilling it, which requires a great deal of work. So does pulling it out of the ground. Additionally, while fires do kill cheatgrass, they must be controlled burns because cheatgrass fires can easily rage out of control. Only experts should try to burn cheatgrass lest the people doing it wind up unintentionally burning large areas of land.

Letting livestock graze on cheatgrass is effective but doesn't work in every situation. After all, uh, animals can't graze everywhere that cheatgrass grows. For instance, livestock aren't allowed on most public lands, so farmers can remove the cheatgrass growing on their land, but, uh, they can't do anything about the public lands adjoining their property. As a result, cheatgrass thrives there and then spreads onto the farmers' lands the following year.

As for herbicides . . . Well, they're effective only at certain times of the year, so they have to be properly managed. They're also expensive, and, you know, they harm the grasses and other plants growing alongside cheatgrass. So, uh, as you can see, there's no single solution to getting rid of cheatgrass. Unfortunately, it appears as though the weed is here to stay for a long time.

Note-Taking

Main Point: methods of eliminating cheatgrass have problems

Argument 1: mowing, tilling, and burning have problems
- plant often grows back if mowed or tilled → have to do again and again
- cheatgrass burns easily → fires can get out of control

Argument 2: livestock not always effective
- can't graze on public land → not allowed
- cheatgrass grows on public land next to farms → next year, spreads to farmers' fields

Argument 3: herbicides limited in effectiveness

- only effective at certain times of year + are expensive
- harm plants and grasses growing alongside cheatgrass

Paraphrasing Exercises

1 People who aren't experts shouldn't burn cheatgrass since the fires could get out of control.

2 Livestock can't go on most public lands, so even if farmers get rid of cheatgrass on their land, it will still be on public lands.

3 They're expensive and hurt plants other than cheatgrass.

C | Combining the Main Points

1 For example, the first proposal is to physically remove cheatgrass by mowing it, tilling it, pulling it up, or burning it. The professor finds fault with these solutions though. She declares that mowing and tilling cheatgrass do not kill it and that pulling it up is labor intensive.

2 The professor disregards the suggestion in the reading passage that farmers should let their livestock, such as cattle, graze on cheatgrass. She remarks that while cows can eat all the cheatgrass in some areas, they cannot go onto adjoining public lands.

3 The professor further challenges the argument in the reading passage that herbicides are useful by mentioning that they kill other plants and grasses, not just cheatgrass.

D | Completing the Essay

Sample Essay

The professor and the author of the reading passage acknowledge that cheatgrass is an invasive species making a nuisance of itself in North America. Yet while the author of the reading passage suggests some ways to eliminate the cheatgrass problem, the professor challenges each argument that is made.

For example, the first proposal is to physically remove cheatgrass by mowing it, tilling it, pulling it up, or burning it. The professor finds fault with these solutions though. She declares that mowing and tilling cheatgrass do not kill it and that pulling it up is labor intensive. As for using fires, she comments that cheatgrass burns easily, so burning it is difficult because the fires can get out of control.

The professor disregards the suggestion in the reading passage that farmers should let their livestock, such as cattle, graze on cheatgrass. She remarks that while cows can eat all the cheatgrass in some areas, they cannot go onto adjoining public lands. What happens is that cheatgrass grows well on those public lands and then spreads to the farmers' lands the next year.

As for herbicides, the professor explains that they are

useful only for a part of the year. She further challenges the argument in the reading passage that herbicides are useful by mentioning that they kill other plants and grasses, not just cheatgrass.

iBT Practice Test

Sample Notes — READING

Goats are good for targeted grazing

1 **better than machines**
- don't pollute environment like lawnmowers
- don't break down like machines
- are more cost effective than machines

2 **are versatile**
- eat wide variety of plants, especially ones resistant to cutting and herbicides
- can climb up hills and rocky terrain to eat plants → hard to get to with machines

3 **fertilize ground while eating**
- urinate and defecate → get absorbed into earth
- act as fertilizer

Listening Script

Now listen to part of a lecture on the topic you just read about.

M Professor: Managing plant growth, uh, particularly that of weeds, is a difficult endeavor. Lately, some people have been experimenting by using goats as lawnmowers. Goats, you see, consume grass and weeds, so people don't require lawnmowers and herbicides. But, um, you know what . . . ? While many people think using goats as lawnmowers is a fantastic idea, I say there are some problems.

To begin with, there are no financial savings. Let's see . . . If you have a few acres of land, it'll take a herd of thirty goats approximately three days to clear it, but a few people with lawnmowers can do the same job in several hours. Now, uh, if you rent a herd of goats for three days, you've got to stock water and food for them. That's right. I said food. They need food since they don't get enough nutrition from the plants they consume. So you're going to wind up paying much more money than you expected. Honestly, it would be cheaper to use lawnmowers.

Now, uh, I agree that goats are efficient eaters. In some ways, however, they're too efficient since they eat flowers and other plants you don't want eaten, so they must be closely monitored. Oh, and goats don't eat the grass evenly, so don't expect to see a well-trimmed lawn. Nor will goats go where you want them to. They're stubborn animals that go wherever they want and consume whatever they want.

Finally, goats are messy. They dig into the dirt under the grass to make places to rest, so your land will have plenty of brown spots. And don't forget about their droppings and urine. Your land will smell awful and be unpleasant to walk on for several days until the ground absorbs everything.

Sample Notes — LISTENING

Are many problems using them as lawnmowers

1 no financial savings
- goat herd takes days to cut land
- need to rent for long time + provide food and water for goats

2 are too efficient at eating
- eat flowers and plants people want → must monitor closely
- don't eat evenly
- stubborn → go wherever they want, not where people want

3 are messy
- dig up ground
- droppings and urine → smell bad

Sample Essay

According to the professor, some people use goats as lawnmowers to cut grass and to get rid of weeds these days. Although the reading passage supports using goats for targeted grazing, the professor finds several problems with this practice.

He begins by pointing out that hiring a herd of goats does not save money. This is in opposition to the reading passage, which asserts that renting goats is cheaper than using machines such as lawnmowers. The professor, however, describes some hidden costs such as the need to rent the goats for several days and the necessity of providing food and water for them. He notes that those costs make goats expensive.

While the professor concurs with the reading passage that goats are good at eating all kinds of plants, he claims that they are too good since they eat everything, including plants people want. Thus goats need to be watched carefully. He adds that goats are stubborn and only go where they want to, so they do not trim yards evenly.

The author of the reading passage points out that goat urine and feces fertilize the land the goats clear, but the professor remarks that they create bad smells which last for several days. He also comments that goats dig up the ground, so they make a mess while they are grazing.

Chapter 10

A | Reading Passage
p. 88

Outlining

Main Point: skeleton dug up is that of King Richard III

Argument 1: skeleton matches known facts about Richard
- man in 30s and has curved spine
- body has many head wounds → was how Richard was killed

Argument 2: DNA tests
- found 2 descendants of Richards → did mitochondrial DNA test
- matched w/Richard → did tests 3 times to be sure

Argument 3: radiocarbon testing
- person was alive during time when Richard lived
- diet was that of a nobleman

Paraphrasing Exercises

1 The head wounds match up with reports on how Richard died in battle.

2 DNA from the bones matched the two people it was compared to.

3 Tests that were run showed the person ate a rich diet that indicated he belonged to the nobility.

B | Listening Lecture
p. 90

Listening Script

Now listen to part of a lecture on the topic you just read about.

M Professor: Despite modern methods of analysis, proving who old bones belong to isn't as easy as you may think. Let me discuss a case that was publicized a few years back. In 2012, a body was unearthed in Leicester, England, by a group of archaeologists looking for King Richard III, who died in 1485 and was buried near Leicester.

The academics found the body of a man in his thirties with a curved spine and numerous wounds to his body. These facts match what we know about Richard . . . but could also fit someone else. More than 1,000 people died in that battle, so it might not be Richard's body. Plus, uh, the curved spine might have resulted when the body was squeezed into the casket, which was tiny.

Now, uh, DNA tests were done and appear conclusive, but . . . Well, mitochondrial DNA is traced through the female line because it doesn't change over time. Keep in mind that Richard had many male relatives whose descendants would also have the same mitochondrial DNA profile. Let's see . . . His grandmother, Joan Beaufort, had sixteen children and numerous grandchildren, all nobles, and most fought in the Wars of the Roses. So while the DNA from the bones matched the descendants of his sister Anne, it would also match the DNA of Richard's male cousins since they had the same grandmother. So this could be the body of one of Richard's relatives, not Richard himself.

Finally, radiocarbon dating isn't precise as it can only date objects in roughly hundred-year spans. And while other tests proved the person ate foods rare for anyone other than nobles to consume, one of Richard's cousins would have eaten a similar diet. So while the body is definitely that of someone in the royal family, we can't be certain it's that of Richard.

Note-Taking

Main Point: hard to prove who old bones belong to

Argument 1: body might not be Richard's
- could match another person → 1,000+ people died at battle
- curved spine caused by being stuff into tiny casket

Argument 2: can't trust DNA evidence
- mitochondrial DNA in all male relatives was same
- body could be one of Richard's male cousins

Argument 3: other tests aren't precise
- radiocarbon dating only covers 100-year spans
- tests show rich diet but could have been other member of royal family

Paraphrasing Exercises

1 The spine may have curved from the body being squeezed into a tiny casket.

2 The DNA matched the descendants of Anne but would also be the same for Richard's male cousins.

3 Tests showed that the person at a nobleman's diet, which is what Richard's cousins ate.

C | Combining the Main Points p. 91

1 The professor starts by agreeing with the author of the reading passage that the physical characteristics of the body match those of Richard. Yet he says that the body could still belong to another person since many people died in that battle.

2 Next, the professor admits that the DNA evidence cited by the author of the reading passage appears to positively identify the body as Richard's. However, he mentions the fact that mitochondrial DNA was tested. According to the professor, Richard's cousins would have had the same mitochondrial DNA profile, so the body might be one of Richard's relatives.

3 While the author of the reading passage believes the diet proves the body is Richard's, the professor thinks it only

proves that the person was a member of the royal family.

D | Completing the Essay p. 92

Sample Essay

During his lecture, the professor discusses a body found beneath a carpark in Leicester, England. While the author of the reading passage believes that the body belongs to King Richard III, the professor brings up some points that cast doubt on this claim.

The professor starts by agreeing with the author of the reading passage that the physical characteristics of the body match those of Richard. Yet he says that the body could still belong to another person since many people died in that battle. He adds that the spine could be curved because of the way the body was stuffed into the tiny casket.

Next, the professor admits that the DNA evidence cited by the author of the reading passage appears to positively identify the body as Richard's. However, he mentions the fact that mitochondrial DNA was tested. According to the professor, Richard's cousins would have had the same mitochondrial DNA profile, so the body might be one of Richard's relatives.

Lastly, the professor comments that radiocarbon dating cannot provide precise times for objects, and he also talks about the rich diet that the person ate. While the author of the reading passage believes the diet proves the body is Richard's, the professor thinks it only proves that the person was a member of the royal family.

iBT Practice Test p. 93

Sample Notes — READING

Black Death had negative effects on Europe

1 **harmed economy**
- destroyed trade and means of living for Europeans
- people too afraid to go out → didn't work
- trade halted → goods became scarce and prices rose

2 **harmed social life**
- people afraid to come into contact w/others
- farms and villages abandoned
- sense of hopelessness

3 **harmed religious life**
- people turned to church → priests got infected and died
- people lost faith in God and religion

Listening Script

Now listen to part of a lecture on the topic you just read about.

W Professor: While the Black Death destroyed much of

fourteenth-century European society, for those who survived, life actually became better. That's right. I said better. This may sound odd, but Europe actually benefitted from the Black Death. For one, the continent was overpopulated at the time, but the plague killed anywhere between one third and one half of the people living there. Initially, this negatively affected Europe, but, uh, in the end, the reduced population made things better.

How . . . ? Well, for one, it freed the surviving peasants from the land in many places and brought feudalism to an end. With so few laborers to be found, peasants could demand higher wages and travel to places where they could obtain better employment. There was also an increased demand for luxury goods since the survivors decided to enjoy their lives more. This stimulated trade and is considered to have inspired the onset of the Age of Exploration, during which people searched for new trade routes around the world.

Furthermore, uh, the loss of so many people created huge tracts of empty farmland, which, in turn, the surviving peasants could purchase cheaply. There were additionally great changes in medicine and scientific research. When prayers and other spiritual methods failed to stop the plague, men of learning searched for new ways. While they failed to find a cure for the plague, their inquiries into the world of knowledge resulted in countless new discoveries in the centuries after the Black Death ended.

While the plague caused many people to question both God and religion, it also led to the reform of the Church. People began questioning the Church and its practices and started thinking in more secular terms. This helped bring about the Renaissance and the Protestant Reformation, both of which had tremendous impacts on society.

Black Death had some positive effects on Europe

1 **helped peasants**
   – freed them from land + ended feudalism
   – trade stimulated → inspired Age of Exploration as people looked for new trade routes

2 **changes in land, medicine, and science**
   – peasants could buy cheap land
   – made inquiries into medicine and science → many new discoveries

3 **reformed Church**
   – questioned Church and practices → became more secular
   – led to Renaissance and Protestant Reformation

Sample Essay

Both the lecture and the reading passage discuss the effects that the Black Death had on Europe after it ended. The reading passage claims that there were many negative effects, but the professor disagrees and explains how the plague had positive effects on society.

The first point the professor covers is how Europe was affected economically. In contrast to the reading passage, which argues that trade stopped while goods became hard to find, the professor states that peasants earned more money and got better job situations. Furthermore, she credits the Black Death with inspiring Europeans to search for new trade routes, which started the Age of Exploration.

The professor also remarks that people began turning to science in an effort to defeat the plague. This, she believes, resulted in an increase of knowledge that led to many scientific discoveries being made in later centuries. Her argument thus goes against the claim in the reading passage that people turned against academics because they could not find a cure for the disease.

Regarding religion, the writer of the reading passage declares that people turned against the church because they lost faith, so they started living lives of pleasure. But the professor argues differently in stating that the Church was reformed and both the Renaissance and Protestant Reformation occurred after the Black Death ended.

Chapter 01

B | Outlining
p. 101

Sample Outline — Agree

Thesis Statement

In my opinion, the teachers at a school are the most important factors in determining whether or not it is successful.

First Supporting Idea

Topic Sentence:

- Good teachers can provide their students with quality educations.

Supporting Example(s):

- older sister went to school w/bad reputation
- next year, hired better teachers → good educators
- school has good reputation today

Second Supporting Idea

Topic Sentence:

- Teachers can help motivate students and make them want to learn.

Supporting Example(s):

- didn't like math when was younger
- math teacher showed me importance of math → like math now

Third Supporting Idea

Topic Sentence:

- Bad teachers can cause schools to fail in their principal mission, which is to educate students.

Supporting Example(s):

- cousin has bad teachers → hates attending school
- teachers often don't teach → make students study alone

Conclusion

Teachers are clearly of great importance to the success of a school.

C | Completing the Essay
p. 102

Sample Essay — Agree

I agree with this statement. In my opinion, the teachers at a school are the most important factors in determining whether or not it is successful. I feel that way for a couple of reasons.

The first reason is very simple. Good teachers can provide their students with quality educations. When teachers lecture well and make their classes interesting, they can provide students with the information they need to be successful in the future. When my older sister was in high school, she attended a school with a bad reputation. During her first year, she did not learn very much. However, the school hired several new teachers during her second year. Those teachers were outstanding educators, so the students at the school, including my sister, all started learning well. By the time my sister graduated, her school had acquired a reputation for being a great place to get a good education.

A second reason teachers are important is that they can help motivate students and make them want to learn. When I was younger, I did not really care about math as I thought it was hard and boring. Then, one year, my math teacher suddenly got me interested in learning the subject by showing me how important math is and teaching me some great ways to learn it. Thanks to him, I started trying harder in math, and I am even a member of my school's math club now.

A third reason is that bad teachers can cause schools to fail in their principal mission, which is to educate students. One of my cousins hates attending school because many of her teachers are terrible and do not even teach half the time. Instead, they just tell the students to read their books and to study by themselves. Unsurprisingly, that school has an awful reputation, and lots of its students are trying to transfer to other places.

Teachers are clearly of great importance to the success of a school. Good teachers can both provide their students with excellent educations and motivate them to do better while bad teachers can cause schools to fail because of their inability or unwillingness to teach their students. I cannot think of any factor more important to the success of a school than the teachers that work at it.

Sample Essay — Disagree

I believe teachers are important to schools, but I do not agree with the statement. I do not think that the success of a school depends upon its teachers for a few reasons.

First of all, most teachers are not really that important to the learning process. For the most part, my teachers only repeat the information that is contained in the books. For instance, there is virtually no reason for me to attend my history class if I read the day's lesson in the textbook before class begins. The reason is that my history teacher just reads from the book and then asks us a few questions. Even though he is a poor teacher, history is my favorite subject, and I feel like I am learning the topic. I simply do not need my teacher though.

Another reason is that schools with modern facilities have little need for teachers. Many schools these days have computer laboratories where students can access the Internet, and they have libraries and science labs, too. So students can get most of the information they need from the Internet. They can read books in their school libraries, and they can conduct experiments in their science labs. That is what my older brother does. He does not pay much attention to his teachers but instead conducts the majority of his learning by himself.

Finally, students who are motivated to study realize that they do not have to depend on their teachers for their educations. My best friend is one of the most self-motivated people I have ever met. She always does extra work that the teachers do not ask for. When she becomes interested in a topic, she studies it as hard as she can by herself. She has gotten perfect grades every year, and she is the top student at my school. But her teachers have had virtually nothing to do with her success. Some of them even tell her that she should slow down and study less.

I disagree with the statement because I believe that teachers do not determine the success of a school. I think other factors, including motivation and modern facilities, are much more crucial to the success of a school than teachers are.

iBT Practice Test
p. 104

Sample Outline — Agree

1   **get older, harder to think → if study, can keep mind sharp**
   - friend's grandfather is 90 → enjoys learning so has keen mind
2   **never too old to learn something new**
   - grandparents are in 70s → enjoy studying
   - grandma studies English w/me & grandpa takes online classes
3   **elderly get bored when retired → get depressed**
   - if study, can get interested in lives

Sample Essay — Agree

There are some people who believe the elderly have no need to study and learn new things, but I am not one of them. Instead, I fully agree with the statement that the elderly ought to study and learn new things.

As people get older, it becomes harder for them to think, and their minds lose focus. By studying, they can keep their minds sharp though. My friend's grandfather is more than ninety years old. However, he is unlike the typical ninety-year-old as he does not just sit around the house and do nothing. Instead, he constantly reads, watches the news, and enjoys learning new things. He has a very keen mind even though he is old, and I love talking to him. Studying has definitely been positive for him.

Second of all, a person is never too old to learn something

new. I often hear old people declare that they are too old to learn to use the Internet or to use some other piece of modern technology. I disagree with them though. My grandparents are in their seventies, but each of them knows how to use a computer and emails me constantly. They also enjoy studying. My grandmother is studying English with me, and my grandfather takes some online business classes. They thoroughly enjoy the time they spend learning and believe it is important to their lives.

A third reason studying and learning are important is that many elderly people are bored since they are retired and mostly stay at their homes. This can cause them to become depressed. Yet if they study or try to learn something new, they get more interested in their lives. They become happier and do not get depressed. I have seen this happen to many elderly people, so I consider learning something they should all do.

It is very important for the elderly to study and learn new things. Doing that can help them keep their minds sharp, it can give them pleasure, and it can keep them from getting depressed. I wish that all older people would try to learn new things. They would enjoy their lives much more if they did that.

Sample Outline — Disagree

1   **if don't work, don't need to study**
   - grandfather studied when was younger
   - doesn't study now → says doesn't need since isn't working
2   **elderly set in ways → don't want to try new things**
   - people in town are farmers → didn't study much when young
   - don't want to start studying now → prefer regular routines
3   **minds get worse as age = have trouble remembering and studying**
   - grandma tried learning computer → got stressed out
   - father got her to stop → felt better

Sample Essay — Disagree

At first glance, the statement seems like something most people would agree with. Nevertheless, after giving this statement some thought, I find that I disagree and do not consider it necessary for the elderly to study and learn new things.

To begin with, most people study and learn to help them do better at their jobs. The vast majority of the elderly do not work though, so they have no need to study. When my grandfather was younger, he studied and learned new things all the time. He is retired now, so he does not study. One day, I asked him why he quit studying, and he responded that he did not have to since he was no longer working.

Another reason is that many elderly people are set in their

ways and do not want to try anything new. I live in the countryside, and many people here are farmers. When they were younger, they did not focus on school but were instead concerned about taking care of their farms. They did that for decades, so they have no interest in changing their lives now. They do not want to begin studying or learning new things since they never did that in the past. Instead, they would prefer to continue with their regular routines.

Something else of relevance to the statement is that as people age, their minds become worse. They have trouble remembering and difficulty studying and learning. Even if they want to learn something new, it can be hard for them. This can give them a great amount of stress, which can therefore lower the quality of their lives. My grandmother tried learning to use a computer, but she could not figure it out, so she got stressed out. My father encouraged her not to do it any longer. After she quit, she felt much better. In her case, learning something new was more harmful than beneficial.

It is not important for the elderly to study or learn new things. Most of them are retired so do not need to study. In addition, the elderly do not like changing their ways, and they can also get stressed out when they try to learn. Therefore, there is no need for the elderly to study or learn anything new.

Chapter 02

B | Outlining

Sample Outline — Agree

Thesis Statement
I believe that it is the government rather than individuals who should pay for the Internet for a few reasons.

First Supporting Idea
Topic Sentence:
– Not everyone can afford to pay for access to the Internet, but the government can.

Supporting Example(s):
– government responsible for taking care of people
– places w/low populations = no Internet infrastructure
– government needs to help them

Second Supporting Idea
Topic Sentence:
– I believe Internet access should be considered a right just like freedom of speech and freedom of religion are rights in many countries.

Supporting Example(s):
– society relies on Internet

– hard to find job w/out Internet
– bro & sis got jobs from online ads → government should help others

Third Supporting Idea
Topic Sentence:
– Too many companies charge expensive rates for Internet access.

Supporting Example(s):
– family lives in small town w/one Internet provider
– has to pay what company charges → excessive $

Conclusion
It is the responsibility of the government to pay for the Internet instead of having individuals do that.

C | Completing the Essay

Sample Essay — Agree

I believe that it is the government rather than individuals who should pay for the Internet for a few reasons. I therefore agree with the statement.

The first reason is that not everyone can afford to pay for access to the Internet, but the government can. As a result, it is the government's responsibility to take care of those unfortunate individuals who cannot pay their monthly Internet bills. This is particularly true in places with low populations. Most Internet providers realize they cannot profit by providing these areas with Internet connectivity, so they never set up any infrastructure for it. Therefore, large numbers of people are deprived of Internet access. If the government were to pay for it though, there would not be any problems.

Furthermore, I believe Internet access should be considered a right just like freedom of speech and freedom of religion are rights in many countries. The reason is that so much of society relies upon the Internet. Consider the importance of the Internet when it comes to finding jobs. It is hard for most people to find employment without access to the Internet. For example, my older brother and sister both got hired thanks to advertisements they saw on the Internet. Since the government ought to promote a good economy, it should pay for everyone's Internet access.

The final issue is that too many companies charge expensive rates for Internet access. This is common in areas with only a couple of Internet providers. My family lives in a small town with one Internet provider, so we have to pay whatever amount of money it charges. That is not fair. People who cannot afford the rate they are being charged are not able to enjoy their lives to the fullest since they are being deprived of Internet access. If the government were to pay for Internet access for everyone, then these companies would not be able to charge excessive rates like they are doing now.

It is clear to me that it is the responsibility of the government to pay for the Internet instead of having individuals do that since not everyone can afford Internet access, Internet access is a right, and many companies overcharge for Internet access. For those three reasons, I strongly agree with the statement.

Sample Essay — Disagree

While I understand why people might support having the government pay for access to the Internet, these individuals are misguided. It is not the government, but people themselves, who should pay for Internet access. I feel this way for a few reasons.

One is that it is not a duty of the government to pay for people's Internet access. The government exists to protect the people it governs from harm. There is nothing in my country's constitution indicating that the government must pay for Internet access for everyone. In fact, the government is already too big, and starting another entitlement program would make it even larger. I am a strong supporter of limited government, so I do not want to see the government involved in a matter like this.

A second reason is that the government in my country is already in serious debt. Last year, the government ran a deficit, and experts are predicting it will do the same thing again this year as well as in the future. Imagine if the government suddenly had to pay for Internet access for millions of people. That would require billions of dollars in increased government spending. That is money the government does not have, so it would go further into debt.

Lastly, I do not believe that access to the Internet is a right. After all, people survived without the Internet for thousands of years. If the Internet were to disappear today, life would be different, but it would not result in wholesale damage to society. If people want access to the Internet, they are more than welcome to pay for it. But those that want it can pay for it while those that do not want it do not have to pay for it. After all, Internet access is an option, not a right. Even though people use the Internet for many reasons, they still need to pay their own money to get access to it.

The government should not pay for people to access the Internet since it should be smaller, the government does not have enough money, and access to the Internet is not a right. On account of those three reasons, I disagree with the statement and instead think that people should pay for their own Internet access.

iBT Practice Test — p. 110

Sample Outline — Agree

1 government must protect cultural heritage

- promotes places to tourists → encourages people to visit
- government is inviting, so should pay for improvements

2 people in traditional places often have little $

- can't afford to pay but government can
- uncle lives in traditional village → government gives him $

3 rules on altering traditional homes

- uncle needs permission to change home
- changes are expensive → government makes laws so should pay for changes

Sample Essay — Agree

I could not agree more with the statement. In my opinion, one of the best ways to attract more tourists is to improve the appearances of old buildings and streets. And I strongly feel that the government should pay for these improvements.

For one thing, it is the government's job to preserve the cultural heritage of the country. My country has a long history, and there are a large number of traditional villages, buildings, and streets all around the nation. The government often promotes these places to domestic and foreign tourists and encourages them to visit these areas. Since the government is inviting people to go to these places, it is only right for the government to pay for the necessary improvements.

In addition, in many instances, the people who live in these traditional places do not have much money, so they cannot afford to pay for improvements to the buildings and local areas. Therefore, the government is obligated to pay for the renovations. One of my uncles lives in a traditional village. Large groups of tourists visit his neighborhood, but he does not make very much money from them, so there is no way that he can afford to pay to take care of the traditional home he owns. Thankfully, the government provides him with some money to make sure his home is in good condition.

Finally, many governments have rules about how the owners of traditional buildings may alter them. For instance, because my uncle lives in an historical home, he is not allowed to make any changes to it without the permission of a government official. When changes are permitted, they require him to hire specialized workers, who are very expensive. Since the government makes such restrictive rules, it is only fair that the government pay for everything.

It is clearly the responsibility of the government to pay to improve the appearances of traditional structures. The government must preserve the country's cultural heritage, the owners of the structures often do not have enough money to pay themselves, and the government's restrictive laws make doing changes expensive. For those three reasons, I agree with the statement.

Sample Outline — Disagree

1 tourism isn't government responsibility

- government doesn't contribute to other industries → shouldn't give to tourism industry

– people wanted government to give $ → citizens said no

2 buildings owned by private individuals
– should pay for own repairs
– don't give my parents $ for home repairs → should give $ to others

3 owners of buildings profit from tourists
– charge admission + sell souvenirs & concessions
– people in tourism industry make lots of $ → don't need government help

Sample Essay — Disagree

I do not agree with the statement because there is no reason for the government to get involved in paying to improve the appearances of old buildings and streets in order to attract more tourists. I have a few reasons for feeling this way.

One is that the tourism industry is not one of the responsibilities of the government. The government exists to keep the country safe from harm, not to favor one industry over another. The government should not contribute money to the automobile industry, the computer industry, or the textile industry, so I do not see why it should pay money to the tourism industry either. A few months ago, some people in the tourism industry suggested that the government pay for renovations to certain buildings, but their suggestion was extremely unpopular in my country. I was pleased many of my fellow citizens felt the same way that I did.

Since these old buildings are owned by private individuals, the owners themselves ought to pay for any improvements to them. The money that my parents and others pay in taxes should not be given to other people to pay for improvements in buildings that those individuals own. After all, the government is not giving any money to my mother and father to repair our house. The reason is that as the owners of the property, it is their responsibility to take care of it and to make it look better. The same is true of the owners of old structures.

A final reason is that the people who own these buildings and other places are the ones who profit when tourists visit them. They not only charge admission, but they also make money by selling souvenirs and concessions. A lot of people in the tourism industry in my country make large amounts of money, so they do not need to receive any more money from the government.

In my opinion, the government has no business paying to improve the appearances of old buildings and streets. It is not the responsibility of the government to pay for private industries. In addition, the structures are privately owned, so the owners should pay for the renovations as they are the ones who are going to profit.

Chapter 03

B Outlining p. 113

Sample Outline — Heavy Fines

Thesis Statement
I believe the perfect way to punish these firms is to impose heavy penalties upon them.

First Supporting Idea
Topic Sentence:
– It is fair for any company that harms the environment to pay for the damage it caused.

Supporting Example(s):
– high penalty can harm company → millions of $
– company caught dumping waste in river → big fine → went bankrupt

Second Supporting Idea
Topic Sentence:
– When the government fines a company for the harm it causes the environment, it can then use the fine money it receives to pay for the cleanup.

Supporting Example(s):
– provides instant $ for cleanup
– taxpayers don't have to pay

Third Supporting Idea
Topic Sentence:
– If companies are fined for their misdeeds, then other businesses will be less likely to engage in similar behavior.

Supporting Example(s):
– heavy fines = deterrents for bad behavior by other companies
– won't want to get fined big $

Conclusion
I consider fines to be the best form of punishment for companies that harm the environment.

C Completing the Essay p. 114

Sample Essay — Heavy Fines

When a company harms the environment through the goods or services it sells, it must be punished. I believe the perfect way to punish these firms is to impose heavy penalties upon them.

The first reason is that it is fair for any company that harms the environment to pay for the damage it caused. This penalty should be extremely high so that it causes great harm to the business. The fine should therefore be for millions or tens of millions of dollars. This will most likely cause the company to lose money and not to make a profit. I remember reading about an incident in which a company was caught dumping toxic waste into a river, which caused a great deal of water pollution. The company was caught and fined millions of dollars. As a result, it later declared bankruptcy and went out of business, which was news I was pleased to read.

When the government fines a company for the harm it causes the environment, it can then use the fine money it receives to pay for the cleanup. There are a couple of advantages to doing this. First, it provides instant money to pay for the affected area to be cleansed. Second, it protects the country's taxpayers from having to pay for the problems caused by the company. A couple of times, businesses in my country contaminated the environment but were not punished. In addition, the government had to pay for the cleanup, which cost billions of dollars. My parents were very displeased that their tax money was being used to pay for problems caused by other people.

A final point is that if companies are fined for their misdeeds, then other businesses will be less likely to engage in similar behavior. So heavy fines can serve as deterrents for bad behavior. Imagine that a company gets fined $100 million for polluting the environment. Other companies in the same industry will be more careful not to create pollution of their own since they will not want to be fined the same amount of money.

Fines can hurt businesses financially, provide money for cleaning up the environment, and serve as deterrents to other companies. For those reasons, I consider fines to be the best form of punishment for companies that harm the environment.

Sample Essay — Other Ways

While fines can be a useful means of punishment, there are other ways to deal with companies that harm the environment. The methods I support would be much better at punishing the firms causing damage while simultaneously ensuring that the environment is returned to its previous condition.

The first method of punishment I support is for any company that damages the environment to be forced to pay for the cleanup no matter what the cost. I do not care if the company goes bankrupt and if the employees, particularly the CEO and other executives, are forced to pay money from their own personal funds. Companies that harm the environment frequently get fined small amounts of money, which is wrong. If they are made to pay for everything to be cleaned up, however, they may be obligated to spend huge amounts of money, which will hurt them financially and prevent taxpayers from having to spend their own money.

Next, if a company produces a product which harms the environment, it should be banned from producing that product anytime in the future. When a company shows that it cannot make something safely and without causing damage,

then it is obviously irresponsible and inept. It is logical that the government stop it from making that particular product. Making my idea a law will keep companies from hurting the environment since they will want to make products that they can profit from.

Finally, when a company damages the environment, its executives should be arrested, put on trial, and, if found guilty, imprisoned. Companies regularly harm the environment, but the people responsible—the CEOs and other executives—almost never get punished. In many instances, they actually get bonuses or are allowed to retire with big pensions. This is a problem around the world. A company in my country poisoned the environment, but nothing happened to the CEO even though he knew the company's factories were releasing harmful pollutants into the atmosphere. He should have been thrown in prison for a long time.

It is obvious that there are better ways of punishing those who cause damage to the environment than fines. Some methods are making those who damage the environment pay for its cleanup, banning companies from producing certain products, and jailing those individuals leading companies that harm the environment.

iBT Practice Test   p. 116

Sample Outline — Raising Prices

1 **people will use less gas and electricity if price is high**
   - if millions use less gas, coal, and oil, can save lots
   - gas price went up → parents drove less often → others did same thing

2 **people who use lots of gas and electricity ought to pay higher prices**
   - people drive big cars → don't care about environment
   - no interest in conserving environment → should be punished w/higher prices

3 **people will demand cheaper forms of energy**
   - will spend $ researching alternative energy → solar, geothermal, & hydroelectric
   - countries will be nuclear power plants → clean and cheap

Sample Essay — Raising Prices

I do not believe we should spend money on trying to come up with alternative forms of energy. Instead, it is my opinion that we should conserve energy by increasing the prices of gasoline and electricity. There are three primary reasons why I believe this.

The first reason is that by raising the prices of gasoline and electricity, people will use less of it. If millions of people act in that manner, large amounts of gas, coal, and oil can be saved over a long period of time, which will help conserve the

Earth's fossil fuels. Higher prices are definitely effective. Last summer, the price of gasoline rose considerably. My parents started driving less often, so we took the bus and subway more. I noticed that many buses and subway cars were full of people, so it appeared that other people were acting the same way as us.

The second reason is that people who use lots of energy in the form of gasoline and electricity should be made to pay higher prices for it. I often see wealthy people driving big SUVs and other cars that get poor gas mileage. These people apparently have no interest in conserving energy, so they should be punished for their attitudes. If we increase the prices of energy, they will have to pay more money for their selfish acts when they waste fossil fuels.

The third reason is that higher energy prices will result in people demanding that cheaper forms of energy be discovered. This means that millions of dollars will be spent on research to try to make alternative forms of energy, such as solar, geothermal, and hydroelectric power, more efficient and less expensive. It will also cause countries to build more nuclear power plants, which can produce cheap and clean electricity.

Raising the prices of gasoline and electricity is the best way to encourage people to conserve energy. People will use less energy to save money. Those whose behavior does not change will have to pay for their actions. And more money will be spent developing other forms of energy. Those three results will all occur if the prices of gasoline and electricity are increased.

Sample Outline — Alternative Energy

1 **can make more efficient**
   - do research on many alternative energy types
   - make solar power and others more efficient → reduce reliance on fossil fuels

2 **alternative energy types = better for environment than fossil fuels**
   - don't pollute + renewable
   - have infinite supply of them

3 **can stop harming environment if don't need fossil fuels**
   - no mining + no more oil spills
   - energy will be cheap and plentiful for everyone

Sample Essay — Alternative Energy

My opinion is that we ought to invest money into improving alternative energy sources rather than increasing the prices of gasoline and electricity. I have a few reasons for feeling this is a better way to encourage energy conservation.

To begin with, if we spend more money on alternative sources of energy, we can make them more efficient. Currently, we get electricity from alternative energy sources such as solar, hydroelectric, geothermal, wind, and nuclear

power. Unfortunately, these forms of energy are not as efficient as they could possibly be. This is especially true of solar energy, which has enormous potential. Researchers could use the extra funding that could be provided to them to discover ways to make solar power and other alternative types of power more efficient, which would enable us to reduce our reliance upon fossil fuels for energy.

A second advantage is that alternative sources of energy are much better for the environment than burning coal, oil, or gas is. Alternative energy sources are clean, so they do not pollute the environment. They are also renewable, so, unlike fossil fuels, which we will are quickly running out of, we have an infinite supply of solar, wind, and water power. We simply need to learn how to harness these energy sources to make them better than they are at present.

A final advantage is that, if we make these energy sources more effective, we can dramatically change the future. If we do not need oil, gas, and coal anymore, we can stop harming the environment as there will be no need to mine or drill for fossil fuels. There will not be oil spills that cause damage to the land and water anymore as well. In addition, energy will become cheap and plentiful, and billions of people around the world will be able to improve their standards of living.

Alternative energy sources are the way of the future. They are better, cleaner, and cheaper than fossil fuels and can improve people's lives a great deal, but we need to spend money on researching them to make those things happen.

Chapter **04**

B | **Outlining**  p. 120

Sample Outline — Sports

Thesis Statement
I vote to support sports over arts and volunteering.

First Supporting Idea
Topic Sentence:
- Sports are among the most popular extracurricular activities at most universities.
Supporting Example(s):
- bro & sis play → have lots of fun
- many students do → university obligated to support

Second Supporting Idea
Topic Sentence:
- Universities are not only places where students go to improve their minds, but they are also places where they can improve their bodies.

Supporting Example(s):
- bro & sis gained weight → played sports & lost weight

– got interested in being healthy → do sports, jog, & lift weights now

Conclusion

Sports need to be funded at the school due to the effect they can have on so many students.

C | Completing the Essay
p. 120

Sample Essay – Sports

It is unfortunate that the university is suffering from a lack of funds and can only support one activity since each of them is worthy. But because a choice must be made, I vote to support sports over arts and volunteering. There are two main reasons why I think it is crucial to support sports.

The first reason is that sports are among the most popular extracurricular activities at most universities. Not only do many universities have sports teams with student-athletes playing on them, but at many schools, more than fifty percent of the student body participates in intramural sports. My brother and sister are currently university students, and they play sports at their schools. My brother plays intramural basketball while my sister participates in intramural soccer and softball. Both of them tell me how much fun they have playing those sports, and they have also mentioned that their schools have other intramural leagues which numerous other students participate in. Because so many students play sports, the university has an obligation to support this popular activity.

Universities are not only places where students go to improve their minds, but they are also places where they can improve their bodies. Playing sports can get people into good shape and make them healthier. My brother and sister gained several kilograms during their freshman years. They lived fairly unhealthy lifestyles and were overweight until they started playing sports. After that, they lost weight and became more interested in being healthy, too. In addition to participating in intramural sports, they jog and visit their schools' weight rooms, which helps them stay in shape. Since students spend the majority of their time on campus, the university ought to support sports and enable them to get into good shape.

I wish the school could provide funding for all three activities, but since it cannot, the choice is clear: Sports need to be funded at the school due to the effect they can have on so many students. Sports can enable students to participate in intramural sports and to have fun, and they can also allow students to improve their health.

Sample Essay – Art

The university has a tough choice to make. It must choose between supporting sports, art, and volunteering. I like all three options, but I believe the school ought to fund art if it can only afford to pay for one of them. Let me explain why I feel that way.

One reason is that supporting art will let students create works of art that can then be displayed on campus. School can be stressful for students, but viewing art that is being exhibited can help them relieve their stress. I recently visited a university campus to see my cousin at her school. She took me on a tour and showed me some art that had been made by the students there. I was impressed by the quality of the art, and I also noticed that there were a large number of students at the exhibition who were admiring the art. These students did not look as stressed out as the students whom I saw walking around campus with backpacks full of books.

Another factor to consider is that private art lessons are expensive. But if the university provides funding for art, talented students can take lessons either for free or at discounted prices. Perhaps a poor, yet talented, student could benefit from the university spending money on art, and that student might later become a great artist such as Michelangelo or Raphael. Even if the student does not become an artist as talented as those Renaissance masters, it is possible that the student could have his or her raw talent transformed into something more focused, which would enable him or her to create outstanding works of art.

In my opinion, the university simply must support art over the other two choices. Doing so will enable students at the school both to create works that they can display for the benefit of the other students on campus and also to get to take art lessons. Those two reasons can benefit a large percentage of the student body, so that is why the university should opt to fund art.

iBT Practice Test
p. 122

Sample Outline – Cleaning a Park

1 **want a clean park to visit**
   – is park in neighborhood → is dirty because not many custodians + people litter
   – would love to clean park → make it beautiful and popular

2 **park = place where people spend leisure time**
   – like going to park w/friends and family → so do others
   – if clean, can benefit self and others

Sample Essay – Cleaning a Park

If I had to choose between those three options, I would select cleaning a park as my community service. I would

32 Part B

choose to do that for two specific reasons.

The first one is that I enjoy going to parks, so I would like to have a clean park to visit. There is a nice park in my neighborhood. It has a big field, a pond, some walking paths, and tennis courts. However, it is not nearly as popular as it could be because it is not particularly clean. My city does not have enough money to pay for full-time custodians to take care of the park, and many local residents, especially teenagers, litter in the park. This results in the park looking run down and dirty. The facilities need to be improved, and the garbage on the ground needs to be picked up and thrown away. I would love to join a group of students dedicated to keeping the park clean. We could beautify the park and make it popular with people.

There is a second reason I would choose to clean a park. A park is a place where local residents can spend their time engaging in leisure activities. People can walk, play sports, exercise, have picnics, and just spend time with their families at parks. I go to my local park with my friends and family and enjoy doing various activities there. So if I helped clean the park, I would not only be doing something that could benefit myself, but I would also be doing something that could benefit a large number of people. Through my small actions of cleaning up trash, many people's lives could improve. I think that would be an efficient use of my time.

If I did some community service, cleaning a park would be my choice. I could improve the park both so that I could use its facilities and also so that other people could utilize its facilities.

Sample Outline — Planting Flowers and Trees

1 **love hometown so want to beautify it**
   - if plant trees and flowers, others will like city too
   - plant different kinds of flowers in different seasons → make trees line streets
2 **flowers and trees → have positive effect on environment**
   - prevent soil erosion → anchor soil to ground w/roots → doesn't get blown or washed away
   - purify air → remove pollutants = people breathe cleaner air

Sample Essay — Planting Flowers and Trees

All three of the choices for community service are appealing to me, but I would be the most interested in planting flowers and trees throughout my city. I can think of two reasons why I would enjoy doing that the most.

First of all, I love my city very much, so it would bring me a great deal of pleasure to beautify it by planting flowers and trees in it. I have lived in my hometown my entire life and have strong feelings toward it. I want other people—both residents and visitors—to like my hometown as well, and that could happen if some students were to start planting

flowers and trees in the area. We could plant different kinds of flowers depending upon the season, and we could plant trees to line some of the streets in the city. That would make my hometown look much better than it currently does.

Another thing to consider is that flowers and trees can have positive effects on the environment, so we should plant as many of them as possible. Flowers and trees can help prevent soil erosion. They do this by anchoring soil to the ground with their roots, so they would be able to prevent valuable topsoil from being blown away by the wind or washed away by water. In addition, many flowers and plants can help purify the air by removing pollutants from it. The more plants there are in an area, the cleaner the air is. In other words, I could enable the people in my city to breathe cleaner air, which would make them healthier and reduce their chances of getting certain respiratory diseases.

The best choice for me would be to plant flowers and plants in my city. I could make my city look nicer, and I could also improve the environment in my city. Thus my actions would provide benefits for both residents and visitors in my city.

Chapter **05**

B | Outlining
p. 125

Sample Outline — Agree

Thesis Statement
The vast majority of successful people are similar to others, so I must agree with the statement.

First Supporting Idea
Topic Sentence:
- In my culture, it is crucial for people to get along well with one another to achieve social harmony. The easiest way to accomplish that is to be similar to others.

Supporting Example(s):
- in my country, is better to be similar to others
- mother is similar to most people → gets along well w/others
- is now VP at company after short time → successful thanks to similarity to others

Second Supporting Idea
Topic Sentence:
- Another way that being similar to others leads to success is that entrepreneurs can better understand what goods and services are appealing to the majority of people.

Supporting Example(s):
- entrepreneurs can understand what appeals to others
- video game designer made popular game
- is typical countryman so just made game he wanted to play → others liked too

Conclusion

It is clear to me that the statement is correct.

C | Completing the Essay

p. 126

Sample Essay — Agree

Some people may claim that those individuals who stand out by being different from the majority of people are successful. While that does happen on occasion, it is uncommon. Instead, the vast majority of successful people are similar to others, so I must agree with the statement.

In my culture, it is crucial for people to get along well with one another to achieve social harmony. The easiest way to accomplish that is to be similar to others. Thus people should have similar likes and dislikes, eat similar foods, dress alike, and even watch the same movies and television programs. Those who are different from the majority of people in my country are regarded as unusual and may occasionally be shunned by people. As a result, it is nearly impossible for them to attain success. On the other hand, people such as my mother can become successful by being similar to others. My mother works at a large manufacturing company in the capital of my country. She is similar to most other people, so that helps her get along well with them. This fact has enabled her to become a vice president at her company in a fairly short period of time. She has achieved success not by being different but by being similar to others.

Another way that being similar to others leads to success is that entrepreneurs can better understand what goods and services are appealing to the majority of people. All they must do is think about what they want to purchase since their likes are similar to those of their fellow citizens. There is a famous video game designer in my country who created a video game that millions of people here enjoy playing. In a recent interview, he was asked how he came up with a game with such broad appeal. He responded that he simply made a game he wanted to play and assumed that others would want to play it, too. He was able to do that successfully since he is a typical person in my country's culture.

It is clear to me that the statement is correct. People can be successful by being similar to others because it enables them to get along with many people and because they can be better for entrepreneurs by understanding the minds of their countrymen more easily.

Sample Essay — Disagree

There are myriad ways for a person to achieve success. An individual does not have to be similar to everyone else to be successful. In fact, a person can be quite different from others. Consequently, I find myself in disagreement with the statement.

Today, one of the easiest ways for a person to succeed in life is to be the first person to do something different from everyone else. For instance, Steve Jobs became an incredibly wealthy man by living his life differently from the majority of people. He dropped out of college and never graduated, and he started a business with a friend by selling personal computers at a time when very few people had them in their homes or even dreamed that they would need them. Apple, his company, became one of the most successful corporations in the world by creating products that were different from those which other companies were making at the time. By being different from others, Steve Jobs attained a level of personal success that few people have ever done.

There are also too many people who simply think like others do, so they lack the ability to think outside the box. However, those rare individuals who are able to look at problems differently from others can find unusual solutions, many of which can result in them being highly successful individuals. Pablo Picasso was someone who could think outside the box. He was already a great artist when he started experimenting with new forms of art. Due to his actions, he devised the form of art known as Cubism. His Cubist works are widely cited as great examples of art, and Picasso himself is considered one of the best artists of the twentieth century. It was his differences from, not his similarities to, others which enabled him to achieve so much success.

Steve Jobs and Pablo Picasso are just two examples of people who acted and thought differently from others and were accordingly able to achieve a great amount of success in their lives. I therefore do not believe that the statement is correct, so I disagree with it.

iBT Practice Test

p. 128

Sample Outline — Agree

1 **great leaders can't know everything**
   - so should be willing to listen to others
   - president has advisors → give advice
   - good president follows advice but bad president doesn't

2 **many leaders lack intelligence but know that**
   - so listen to smart advisor
   - CEO at father's company not smart → is charismatic
   - listens to advisors → uses charisma to get others to follow him

Sample Essay — Agree

Great leaders are not always individuals who can do everything by themselves. Sometimes they have to rely upon others for assistance. I therefore agree with the statement and believe that great leaders should listen to the opinions of other people.

Something which all great leaders should realize is that

they cannot know everything. For that reason, they ought to be willing to listen to people who know more about certain topics, and then the leaders should follow the advice those experts give. For example, the president of a country does not make decisions only according to what he or she knows. Instead, the president has large groups of advisors who possess specialized knowledge about various topics, including economics, foreign relations, and national security. Those advisors provide the president with knowledge and then usually give advice regarding what ought to be done. When the president follows this advice, things usually work out well. However, many times, when a president disregards the advice and does whatever he or she feels like doing, the president winds up causing problems. That is the sign of a poor leader. A great leader, on the other hand, listens to the advice of experts and follows it.

Secondly, many great leaders realize they may lack the intelligence to understand certain things, so they must utilize smart advisors who can tell them what they ought to do. Then, the leaders can use their charisma to encourage others to follow them and to do their bidding. My father works at a large company with a highly charismatic CEO. The CEO is not particularly intelligent and often tells people that. However, he has assembled a team of advisors who provide him with excellent advice. The CEO almost always follows that advice and then uses his charisma to convince my dad and his coworkers to follow him. This has made my father's company extremely successful. And it happens because the CEO recognizes that he needs to listen to other people for advice.

Great leaders do not just do whatever they want to do. Instead, they should listen to advice from others and then follow it. By doing so, they can become people whom others will be willing to follow.

Sample Outline — Disagree

1 **great leaders = people who do what they want**
- consider objectives → encourage others to follow
- principal decided to improve school → ignored others = success

2 **if people listen to others, are no longer leaders**
- uncle used to lead family well
- became more inclusive → started leading less → family doesn't respect him now

Sample Essay — Disagree

I disagree with the statement that a great leader should listen to the opinions of other people. There are a couple of reasons why I feel this way.

First of all, great leaders are people who do what they want. They do not listen to others and do what those individuals desire. Instead, great leaders consider their objectives and

then encourage people to follow them as they endeavor to achieve their goals. The principal at my school did that. When he arrived at my school two years ago, people had a low opinion of it. He decided to fix the school to make it one that students and parents could be proud of. When he began, many people gave him advice, but he remarked that he had his own ideas and was uninterested in theirs. This upset some people, but the principal's ideas worked, so nearly everyone followed his agenda. Today, the principal is regarded as one of the top educators and greatest leaders in my country. He accomplished that by doing what he wanted, not by following the opinions of others.

Additionally, when people listen to others and follow the advice given by those people, they lose their leadership abilities. After all, they are no longer being leaders but are instead being followers. My uncle is an example of this. His children—my cousins—used to respect him a lot because he was a great leader. He took charge of his family and told everyone what to do, and everyone obeyed him. Then, about two years ago, he got influenced by some websites he visited and changed his style to become more inclusive. That was a big mistake. He started asking for input from his family about major decisions. At first, his wife and children liked this, but then they realized that he was no longer leading the family. Now, they rarely listen to him and do not consider him a person whom they should respect as a leader.

I cannot agree with this statement because I have seen what happens both when people do not listen to others' opinions and when they do listen to others' opinions. Based on my first-hand knowledge, I have come to understand that leaders are people who follow their own advice and move toward their goals by doing what they want to do rather than what other people want them to do.

Chapter 06

B | Outlining
p. 131

Sample Outline — Older Siblings

Thesis Statement
I believe that older siblings need to look after their younger siblings.

First Supporting Idea
Topic Sentence:
- Siblings are closer in age than they are to adults, so they can understand one another much better.

Supporting Example(s):
- siblings = closer in age than parents
- older sis raised me → understood me well
- parents didn't understand me, so sis had to explain to them

Second Supporting Idea

Topic Sentence:

– Older siblings can benefit by raising their younger siblings.

Supporting Example(s):

– older siblings learn leadership + taking care of others

– can mature faster than others same age → my sis

– sis focuses on family + doesn't waste time

Third Supporting Idea

Topic Sentence:

– Siblings can learn to get along much better.

Supporting Example(s):

– siblings get along better

– sis and I never fight → settle problems amicably

– cousins went to day care → fight a lot → dislike going to their home

Conclusion

Older siblings, not parents, should be responsible for taking care of their younger siblings.

C | Completing the Essay

p. 132

Sample Essay — Older Siblings

I imagine that the majority of people would say that parents ought to take care of their young children. I, however, am a member of the minority and believe that older siblings need to look after their younger siblings.

One reason I feel this way is that siblings are closer in age than they are to adults, so they can understand one another much better. Because my parents work, my older sister played a major role in raising me when I was young. She did a much better job than my parents since she understood me so well. She knew what I liked and wanted, and she also understood why I felt that way. Many times, my parents were clueless about my wants and needs, and it was not until my sister explained what I wanted or needed that they understood.

Another reason is that older siblings can benefit by raising their younger siblings. For example, they can learn skills such as leadership, and they can also learn about taking care of others. This can help them grow up faster than others their own age. I have noticed that my sister has a more mature outlook on life than her friends do. She is more interested in her family and does not waste time doing pointless activities. I attribute those characteristics to the fact that she cared for me as a child.

A final reason is that siblings can learn to get along much better. My sister and I have a wonderful relationship and never fight. We might have disagreements on occasion, but we always settle them amicably. On the other hand, my friends who were not taken care of by their older siblings tend to fight constantly. My two cousins attended day care and did not spend much time together while they were growing

up. They fight so much that I dislike visiting their house. It is pretty sad how poorly they get along with each other.

Older siblings, not parents, should be responsible for taking care of their younger siblings. Both the older and younger siblings will benefit from this arrangement, and they will get along better with one another. There are so many advantages to doing this that I am shocked that fewer parents put their older children in charge of looking after their younger ones.

Sample Essay — Parents

I have seen older siblings trying to take care of their younger brothers and sisters, and their efforts seldom ended in success. Meanwhile, whenever parents look after young children, the parents and children almost always benefit. Thus I support having parents look after their young children.

The first reason is the most obvious one: Parents have many skills they can teach their children, and they can best do this by looking after their children. When I was young, my mother took care of me and taught me many things in the process. My mom is a housewife, so she often had help with the household chores. I learned to clean, cook, sew, and do other similar activities. My mother also helped me with my schooling, so I got excellent grades at school, too.

Additionally, when parents take care of their children, it can enable the two of them to form close bonds that will last a lifetime. My father also assisted in raising me alongside my mother. I feel a very close connection to my parents. For instance, I have noticed that many of my friends are embarrassed to go out in public with their parents. In contrast, I do not mind being seen by others with my parents and actually prefer their company to that of most of my friends and acquaintances.

Yet another advantage of having parents raise their young children is that the parents will be enough of a positive influence on their children to enable them to grow up to be responsible adults. Too often, parents do not get involved in raising their children but instead drop them off at daycare centers or tell their older siblings to look after them. Then, those children grow up to be poor adults. They cause problems and get in trouble with the law. But when parents take care of their children, the children typically become well-adjusted young men and women and have a greater chance of success in their lives.

When parents look after their own young children, they can teach their children well, form strong bonds with them, and increase their children's chances of becoming successful adults. For those three reasons, I think that it is better for children to be raised by their parents rather than by their younger siblings.

Sample Outline — Move Out

1 **graduate from high school → legally adult so should act like adult**
   – cousin moved out → doesn't depend on parents for anything
   – friend's bro stayed home → graduated 10 years ago, but no job and gets $ from parents

2 **become independent**
   – cousin never takes $ from parents → pays for everything
   – depends on no one for well-being = freedom

3 **can experience life on own so grow up faster**
   – learn to pay bills or suffer consequences
   – can mature more quickly → better able to handle other challenges

Sample Essay — Move Out

When children graduate from high school, one of the first things they should do is move out of their parents' homes and begin the next chapter in their lives. They ought to do this for a few important reasons.

For starters, when most students graduate from high school, they are old enough to be legally considered adults, so they need to start acting like adults. The best way to do that is to move out of their parents' homes and to start their own lives. When my cousin graduated from high school several years ago, she moved into her own place almost immediately. She stated she wanted to be an adult and did not want to depend on her parents for anything. Meanwhile, the older brother of one of my friends is still living with his parents even though he graduated from high school ten years ago. He does not work, so his parents give him money. He does not act like an adult at all.

Another reason high school graduates should move out is that they need to become independent, and living away from one's parents is one of the best ways to attain freedom. My cousin has never accepted any money from her parents since she graduated from high school. She has always paid her rent with her own money, and she pays the bills and groceries with the money she earns from working as well. Since she depends on nobody for her own well-being, she is living a life of freedom that I really envy.

Last of all, moving out lets high school graduates experience life on their own, so they can grow up much faster. They learn that bills have to be paid on time and in full, or else they will suffer the consequences. If they manage to pay their bills and do not have to ask their parents for money, they will mature more quickly and will be better able to handle the other challenges they will face in their lives.

High school students should be sure to move out of their

homes as quickly as possible after they graduate. They need to start acting like adults by showing their independence, and they can also mature much faster. It will benefit them greatly if they get out and live away from their parents.

Sample Outline — Stay until Married

1 **can save $**
   – sis lives at home after graduating → no rent, utilities, or groceries
   – saves most of $ → will help when gets married

2 **get support from parents while focusing on careers**
   – sis very tired when came home → didn't do chores
   – focused on job so got promoted quickly

3 **learn to act like adults → can learn from parents**
   – sis watched parents → started acting like them
   – gets up early + doesn't waste $

Sample Essay — Stay until Married

I can understand the appeal of moving out of one's parents' home after graduating from high school, but I have no interest in that myself. In fact, I believe children should live with their parents until they get married, and then they can move out.

To begin with, by living at home, a person does not have to rent or buy a new place, so it is cheaper. Since the economy is not particularly good these days, saving money is of great importance. My older sister graduated from high school about eight years ago, and she still lives at home. She has a job but does not pay rent or utilities, nor does she buy groceries either. Thus she is saving most of the money she earns at her job, which will help her tremendously when she gets married in the future.

Secondly, after graduating from high school, many young adults try to start their careers. By living at home, they can get support from their parents while they are working at the same time. When my sister landed her first job, she was exhausted when she arrived home every day. Fortunately for her, she did not have to cook, clean, or do other household tasks, but she could instead focus on her job. She did her duties so well that she got promoted within a year. I believe living at home enabled her to do that.

Thirdly, just because high school graduates may legally be adults does not mean they know how to act like adults. If they continue to live at home with their parents, they can learn from their mother and father how to behave properly. My sister closely observed my mother and father and began acting like them in many ways. For instance, she now gets up early like both of them and does not waste money like she used to when she was younger. It is obvious how much of an influence my parents have had over her during her adult life.

Living at home until marriage is a much better option than moving out after graduating from high school. Young adults can save money, focus on their careers, and learn how to be an adult by staying at home. Staying in one's parents' home is the best move a high school graduate can make.

Chapter 07

B | Outlining

p. 137

Sample Outline ― Do Homework

Thesis Statement

As long as people are in school, they should do their homework after school is done for the day.

First Supporting Idea

Topic Sentence:
– Homework is an integral part of the education process, so students can complete their educations by doing it.

Supporting Example(s):
– is part of education process
– are benefits → can reinforce what learned + acquire new knowledge
– don't complain about homework since will give me good education

Second Supporting Idea

Topic Sentence:
– Doing homework can also help students prepare for the future.

Supporting Example(s):
– can prepare for future
– teachers assign essays to write → preparation for writing reports at job in future
– if do lots of writing now, can be better prepared for future

Third Supporting Idea

Topic Sentence:
– Students can learn a great deal about responsibility by doing homework.

Supporting Example(s):
– learn about responsibility
– must do math homework every day
– have long-term assignments → become more responsible by doing

Conclusion

While I do not always enjoy doing homework, I appreciate how important it is, so I believe students ought to focus on it after school.

C | Completing the Essay

p. 138

Sample Essay ― Do Homework

As long as people are in school, they should do their homework after school is done for the day. Doing that would be much better than choosing to do other types of activities.

Homework is an integral part of the education process, so students can complete their educations by doing it. Even though students often complain about having too much homework, most of them recognize the obvious benefits. They can reinforce what they learned in their lessons, and they can acquire new information as well. Sometimes I think my teachers give me too much homework, but I try not to complain about it. I keep quiet because I know homework is necessary for me to get the best education possible.

Doing homework can also help students prepare for the future. For example, my teachers regularly have their students write essays or reports for homework. Writing them is difficult, but I realize that I am being prepared for when I have a job in the future. I know I will likely need good writing skills as well as the ability to write convincing essays or reports for whatever job I have. By doing lots of writing homework now, I can be better prepared for the future when I have to do the same thing when I am working.

Students can learn a great deal about responsibility by doing homework, too. I have math homework nearly every day, so I must consistently solve around ten math questions daily, or I will get a zero on my homework assignment. In addition, other teachers give me bigger assignments that may take a few weeks to do. I learn about being responsible for completing long-term projects thanks to these assignments.

While I do not always enjoy doing homework, I appreciate how important it is, so I believe students ought to focus on it after school. Doing homework permits students to get good educations, helps them prepare for the future, and teaches them responsibility. Those are three important benefits which all students can gain from.

Sample Essay ― Choose Other Activities

In my opinion, students should not be forced to do their homework after school but should be allowed to choose to do other activities if they desire to. Students who get to select their activities will be advantaged in several ways.

I am a big supporter of freedom and do not enjoy telling others what to do, so I think students should be permitted to choose what they would like to do after school. If students want to study, then they should be free to do so. But those who want to do something different should be allowed to do that as well. Students should be able to play sports, learn a new language, play a musical instrument, sit at home and watch television, or do anything else they feel like doing. The freedom to choose should be given to them.

We should also consider that not all students are interested in school or good at it, so they should not be forced to do homework. Several of my friends are simply not good at school, so they hate doing homework. They would much rather be playing the piano, painting, or playing basketball. They would be much happier if they could do those activities, so I believe their parents should permit them to do those things.

Parents should remember that students can become successful even if they do not study all the time. There are many ways to become a success; doing well at school is merely one of them. But students need to be happy to become successful, so they should not be obligated to do homework. Instead, they should be encouraged to do whatever they believe will lead them to success. My brother always did poorly at school, so my parents let him focus on his hobby. Today, he is a successful photographer thanks in part to the countless pictures he took when he could have been doing his homework.

Not all students like school or do well at it, so they should be allowed to choose what activities they do after school. They will become happier and may find a new path to success thanks to the freedom they are given to choose their own activities.

iBT Practice Test

p. 140

Sample Outline — Improve the Quality of Food in the Cafeteria

1 **students growing so need lots of nutritious food**
   - improve food quality → students are healthier so won't get sick & miss school
   - students that eat nutritious food don't get sick much
   - students that eat junk food get sick a lot

2 **if eat healthy meals, can concentrate better**
   - eat good meal → can think more clearly & concentrate
   - eat candy bar → don't feel like that

3 **students often hate cafeteria food so dislike school**
   - if tastes better, students will like → will enjoy school
   - friends & I get happy when see good food on menu → could be like that every day

Sample Essay — Improve the Quality of Food in the Cafeteria

The function of a school is to provide each of its students with the best possible education during school hours. For that reason, ensuring that the food in the cafeteria is improved in quality is much more important than paying for students to take part in extracurricular activities.

Elementary school students are still growing, so they need as much nutritious food as they can eat. By improving the quality of the food, the students will become healthier.

That, in turn, will enable them to study better since they will miss fewer days of school by being sick. I have noticed that students who eat nutritious food are almost never sick whereas those that love junk food get sick constantly. If the school cafeteria provides high-quality food, the school will be full of healthy students.

When students eat healthy meals, they are better able to focus on whatever they are doing. This means the students will be able to concentrate on their lessons, especially in the afternoon. When I eat a good meal, I am able to think more clearly and can concentrate well, but when I eat a candy bar, I do not feel the same way. It would be ideal if the students could focus more on their lessons by eating quality food.

Another point to consider is that students often hate the food served in cafeterias, which causes them to dislike school. If the food improves in quality, it will most likely taste better, so the students will like eating it. That, in turn, will make them enjoy school more. My friends and I become happy when we see certain foods on the cafeteria menu. We eagerly talk about the food and actually look forward to eating lunch on that day. Imagine how happy the students would be if they were enthusiastic about having lunch at the cafeteria every day.

The school should definitely pay to upgrade the quality of food since it will result in healthier, happier students who pay closer attention to their lessons. That will make the school much better since the students will perform well in their classes.

Sample Outline — Pay for Extracurricular Activities

1 **can learn new skills**
   - took art lessons after school + learned to play flute
   - learned a lot → still use skills today

2 **students spend more time w/classmates → become good friends**
   - improve social skills → interact w/others
   - was shy when started flute → made good friends so became talkative

3 **activities are fun**
   - students can become happier
   - looked forward to art and music lessons
   - other students love practicing and playing sports

Sample Essay — Pay for Extracurricular Activities

If the school has extra funds to spend, it absolutely must use the money on extracurricular activities that the students can participate in after the school day comes to an end. There would be several benefits from doing this.

One benefit is that the students will have the opportunity to learn new skills. Schools nowadays offer various kinds of extracurricular activities, the most popular of which are sports, art, and music. When I was in elementary school, I took art lessons after school, and I also learned to play the flute. I learned a tremendous amount about art and music by doing those activities, and so did my classmates who participated in those lessons. Since elementary school, I have continued to draw and to play the flute, so I have been using the skills I learned then.

A second benefit is that students who participate in extracurricular activities will spend more time with their classmates and become better acquainted with them. That will not only help them become better friends, but it will also improve the students' social skills because they will have to interact with others on a regular basis. When I first began learning to play the flute, I was shy and disliked speaking with others. However, I made some good friends during my music lessons, and they helped me become more talkative and outgoing.

A final point to consider is that extracurricular activities are frequently fun, so the students will be able to participate in activities they enjoy, which will make them happier. I always looked forward to the days when I had art or music lessons after school. And I know that students who play sports are eager to practice or to play games once school ends. If the school sponsors some extracurricular activities, it will definitely have a happier student body.

Spending money on extracurricular activities is the obvious choice. The students who participate in them will learn new skills, spend more time with their classmates, and enjoy doing those activities. For those reasons, the school should definitely utilize the extra money on extracurricular activities.

Chapter 08

B | Outlining

Sample Outline — Agree

Thesis Statement
I consider it much better to have an intelligent friend, so I agree with the statement.

First Supporting Idea
Topic Sentence:
– You can talk to an intelligent person about many different subjects.

Supporting Example(s):
– can talk about many subjects
– best friend is smart → have discussions about many topics
– never boring to meet her

Second Supporting Idea
Topic Sentence:
– An intelligent friend is also able to help you solve any

problems you have.

Supporting Example(s):
– can solve problems
– if have problem, tell smart friend → can solve
– had problem w/mother → smart friend provided solution that worked

Third Supporting Idea
Topic Sentence:
– An intelligent friend can give good advice on a variety of topics.

Supporting Example(s):
– can give good advice
– didn't know what to do for summer → spoke to smart friend
– did pros and cons of choices → gave good advice so had great summer

Conclusion
While I do not always enjoy doing homework, I appreciate how important it is, so I believe students ought to focus on it after school.

C | Completing the Essay

Sample Essay — Agree

It might be fun to have a friend with a good sense of humor, but I do not think it is very important. I consider it much better to have an intelligent friend, so I agree with the statement.

The first reason is that you can talk to an intelligent person about many different subjects. My best friend is quite intelligent, so I love talking to her. She is knowledgeable about topics such as current events, history, economics, and science. Those are subjects that interest me as well, so we usually have great discussions whenever we meet. It is never boring talking to my best friend because there are so many different issues we can converse about.

Furthermore, an intelligent friend is also able to help you solve any problems you have. Anytime there is a problem in my life, I make sure to tell one of my smart friends about it. That friend can almost always solve the problem in a fairly simple manner. Once, I had a serious problem with my mother, and I told a smart friend about it. He promptly explained to me how I could solve the problem. Since he is intelligent, I did exactly what he told me to do, and his solution worked.

Finally, an intelligent friend can give good advice on a variety of topics. Last summer, I was not sure what I should do during vacation. I was contemplating studying a few academic subjects or staying at my grandparents' home in the countryside for a few weeks. My best friend sat down and talked with me about the pros and cons of doing each. She advised me to visit my grandparents but to take some study material with me. I followed her advice and had a great summer during which I learned a lot and got closer to my grandparents.

An intelligent friend is better to have than a friend with a good sense of humor. A smart friend can discuss many topics, solve problems, and give good advice. I believe I am fortunate because I have some intelligent friends who can do all three of those things for me.

Sample Essay — Disagree

It might be nice to have an intelligent friend, but it is not more important to have a smart friend than one with a sense of humor. In fact, I would prefer to have a friend who is funny.

A friend with a sense of humor can make you laugh. Laughter is such an important part of life but is something that many people ignore. I see so many people who are overly serious. They focus only on their educations, jobs, families, or other similar things. They are important, but those individuals are missing out on the opportunity to enjoy their lives. One great way to have fun is to laugh. One of my close friends has a great sense of humor, so he always makes me laugh and does a wonderful job of preventing me from taking life too seriously.

A second advantage to having a friend with a sense of humor is that that kind of person may look at things from a different point of view. For instance, the other day, I got a horrible grade on one of my tests at school. I was depressed about it until my funny friend commented, "Well, it looks like you'll never have a career as a chemist." It was funny, so it made me laugh, but it was also true. I am terrible at chemistry, so I now realize that I should focus on studying subjects other than it. My friend's unique way of looking at things helped me make an important life choice.

Funny friends are good to have around when you are sad because the best way to change your mood when you are feeling down is to start laughing. People who are funny have a knack for cheering people up and making them feel better. They can help you take your mind off whatever is bothering you and make you happier. I cannot count the times that my friend with a great sense of humor has done that for me. I am much happier when he is around.

A friend with a sense of humor is much better than an intelligent friend. A funny friend can make you laugh, may have a unique way of looking at things, and can cheer you up when you are sad. For those reasons, I disagree with the statement.

Sample Outline — Agree

1 **have gotten knowledge from school friends**
   - go over material after school → expand upon learning
   - teachers say we know a lot → got knowledge thanks to friendship

2 **learned about concepts such as friendship, honesty, & loyalty**
   - learned to treat people and to behave properly
   - am loyal, trustworthy, & dependable thanks to friends

3 **learned about life in general**
   - have had good and bad experiences w/friends → have learned about life
   - are good times and bad times w/friends and in life

Sample Essay — Agree

I strongly agree with the statement because I have learned a large number of things from my friends. In fact, I would say that I have learned more from my friends than I have from my parents and teachers.

For one thing, I have acquired a tremendous amount of knowledge from my friends at school. When my classes are finished, a couple of my friends and I always get together and go over the material we learned that day. After that, we try to expand upon our learning by teaching one another new information related to what we studied in our classes. Many of our teachers have commented that we are very knowledgeable about the subjects we are studying in class. We acquired that knowledge thanks to our close friendship.

I have additionally learned about abstract concepts such as friendship, honesty, and loyalty from my friends. Over the course of many years, my relationships with my friends have taught me how to treat people properly and how to behave around others. I have learned how to be a loyal friend, and I have become trustworthy and dependable, too. I think I have become a better person thanks to these positive traits which I have learned about from my friends.

One last thing that my friends have taught me about is life in general. I have been through both good and bad experiences with my friends. I have had great friendships, and I have had some of my friendships end for various reasons. Through my relationships with my friends, I have learned about life. I know that life is not always positive, nor is it always negative. There are good times and bad times, just like there are with my friends.

It is clear to me that I have learned very much from my friends. I have more knowledge because of them, I have learned various abstract concepts thanks to them, and I have also learned about life from them. My friends have definitely taught me a lot.

1 **mostly just play w/friends**
  – play computer games and sports
  – fun activities but don't learn from them

2 **don't talk much**
  – play computer games → focus on games
  – play sports → don't say much
  – speak little so don't learn

3 **friends aren't academics**
  – get poor grades → don't care about grades
  – don't like learning or reading news → is nothing to learn from them

Sample Essay — Disagree

After considering the statement, I find myself in disagreement with it. For several reasons, I do not believe I have learned many things from my friends.

For the most part, my relationships with my friends only involve playing with them. For instance, my friends and I regularly play video games or sports together after school. We might visit one person's house and sit in front of the computer for a few hours and play games. Or we might go to the playground and play soccer and basketball until the sun goes down. While those activities are fun, I would not say that I have actually learned anything from them.

Secondly, my friends and I do not talk to one another very much. When we are playing computer games, we are focused on the action in the games themselves. Likewise, we do not say much when we are playing soccer or basketball. Since we are speaking infrequently, we are not learning from one another.

Thirdly, although I like my friends, they are not academically inclined, so there is no way I can acquire any knowledge from them. My friends are fun to hang out with and to play with, but most of them do poorly at school. They frequently receive C's and D's on their report cards, and they do not care about their grades at all. They do not try to learn in class, and they do not read newspapers or visit online news websites. They know virtually nothing that is going on in the world. So I have to speak with members of my family or teachers if I want to acquire that kind of knowledge.

I wish I could say that I have learned many things from my friends, but that would not be a true statement. My relationships with my friends are based on playing together, so we rarely talk to one another. And since my friends do not care much about school, I do not learn anything from them that is related to knowledge. For those reasons, I disagree with the statement.

Chapter 09

B | Outlining   p. 149

Sample Outline — Agree

Thesis Statement
Video games can definitely help children between the ages of five to eight learn because they will get children interested in certain topics.

First Supporting Idea
Topic Sentence:
– Most children have a hard time paying attention to their teachers in class, but they love video games, so games can make them listen carefully during class.

Supporting Example(s):
– students will pay attention to games
– hard to pay attention in class → love watching games
– little bro loves games → always watches closely → could learn a lot from games

Second Supporting Idea
Topic Sentence:
– Nowadays, we live in an age of technology, of which video games are one aspect.

Supporting Example(s):
– children love games and are good at them
– little bro & cousin love games → learn to play quickly
– could do the same if used games to learn with

Third Supporting Idea
Topic Sentence:
– If teachers use video games, they can add some variety to their lessons, which will capture the students' attention.

Supporting Example(s):
– is boring to listen to teacher and read every day
– can add variety w/video games → capture students' attention
– get students interested in school → learn more

Conclusion
Teachers ought to use video games to teach students who are between five and eight years of age.

C | Completing the Essay   p. 150

Sample Essay — Agree

Video games can definitely help children between the ages of five to eight learn because <u>they will get children interested in certain topics. I therefore agree that teachers should use video games in classes to teach young children.</u>

Most children have a hard time paying attention to their teachers in class, but they love video games, so <u>games can make them listen carefully during class.</u> My little brother cannot stand reading books, but when he sees a person playing a video game, he suddenly watches very closely and focuses on the game. If teachers can find ways to impart knowledge upon their students by utilizing video games, then they should definitely do it. I am positive that students will pay attention and therefore learn from the games.

Nowadays, we live in an age of technology, of which video games are one aspect. Children play video games constantly and are often highly skilled at learning to play them. I seldom play video games, but my little brother and cousin, who are the same age as each other, love them. When they get a new game, they master it within a couple of hours. Imagine if they got to learn by playing games. They would almost surely learn quickly and would probably have a great time doing so.

Most elementary school students do the same thing every day: They listen to their teachers provide instruction and read books. After a while, that becomes boring and monotonous, so they may not be interested in their lessons, especially at the end of the day. However, if teachers use video games, they can add some variety to their lessons, which will capture the students' attention. By doing something different, teachers can get their students more interested in school, and that will encourage students to want to learn more.

Teachers ought to use video games to teach students who are between five and eight years of age. Video games can help students pay attention, they can provide a medium of learning which students are familiar with, and they can break up the monotony of a typical day. I am positive that young students would learn a great deal if teachers were to use video games in their classes.

Sample Essay — Disagree

It seems like it would be fun to teach young students by using video games, but there would be too many problems if teachers used this approach. As a result, I disagree with the statement and believe that teachers should avoid using video games to provide instruction to students.

The main reason is that most children associate video games with fun rather than learning, so they will want to play games and not study at school. Even if there are lessons embedded in the games, the bulk of students will ignore whatever they are being taught and focus their attention on playing the games themselves. My mother bought me some educational games when I was younger, and I learned virtually nothing from them; however, I had a fun time playing the games. That is exactly what would happen if teachers taught their classes with video games.

Another problem is that the students will pester their teachers by asking them to play video games. It will become annoying to teachers when their students constantly interrupt their lessons to ask when they are going to play games. The students will watch the clock carefully until it is game time, so they will not pay attention to their teachers. Then, when the

teachers tell the students it is time to stop playing the games, the students will protest and demand to play longer.

Once students are permitted to play games as a part of their learning experience, they will find book learning boring. Personally, I love using computers to learn, but the more I use computers to study with, the harder I find it to read books. Since most learning at elementary schools is done from books, teachers would be making a big mistake if they started using video games as teaching tools. The students will love the video games but will despise other types of learning, which will result in students learning less at school.

It would be a huge mistake for teachers to use video games to teach young students. The students will be interested in the games rather than learning. They will also continually ask about the games and will become bored with book learning. Thus I disagree with the statement and feel that teachers should avoid using video games as educational materials.

iBT Practice Test   p. 152

Sample Outline — Agree

1 **best schools have outstanding facilities**
   - Harvard → great library → scholars visit to use library system
   - MIT → impressive labs → do research and make inventions

2 **self-motivated students use facilities well**
   - don't need instructors → just find materials or do experiments
   - student built robot → didn't get help from professor → used lab at university

3 **great facilities attract best students and professors**
   - 5 years ago → school began upgrading facilities
   - famous professors wanted to work there → hired new professors

Sample Essay — Agree

Some people claim that famous lecturers make universities great, but I disagree with them. I believe that facilities such as libraries and science laboratories are what make universities great, so I agree with the statement and think that universities should invest the money that they receive in their facilities.

The best schools have outstanding facilities. Harvard University is one of the world's top schools, and it has an amazing library system. Its main library has a vast collection larger than virtually every other library in the world. Scholars love using the Harvard library system because they can get nearly any book they need. In addition, MIT, an excellent research university, has impressive laboratories. The students and faculty members there use the labs to do cutting-edge research and to devise various inventions. Universities that desire to become like Harvard and MIT should invest money into developing facilities to make them as good as possible.

When schools have good facilities, self-motivated students will utilize them to the best of their ability. Those students do not require famous instructors to tell them what to do. Instead, they will simply find the research materials they need at the library or do experiments in a laboratory. I recently read an article about a local student who built a robot at his university. He did it by himself without any help from a professor, but he only accomplished that because of the outstanding laboratory at his university. His school clearly invested its money wisely.

There is also a trickle-down effect when a school has great facilities as it will attract the best students and professors, who will want to make use of those places. Five years ago, a university in my province began buying books for its library and updating the equipment in its laboratories. As its facilities improved, some famous professors applied to work there. The university wound up hiring a few new engineering and chemistry professors solely because its laboratories were among the best in the country. That university managed to get excellent professors thanks to its facilities.

I agree with the statement that universities should opt to invest any money that is donated to them to improve their facilities. Those investments can help them become first-rate schools that will appeal to outstanding students and professors.

Sample Outline — Disagree

1 can stress education
- famous professors good at teaching → can get students to learn a lot
- students more likely to pay attention to famous professors
- sis still talks about class w/famous history professor

2 best students will apply to study with famous professors
- bro is high school senior → thinking about which schools to apply to
- only wants to attend school w/famous instructors

3 students will remember university years fondly
- if schools request donations, will be more likely to give $
- sis always gives $ to school → maybe 1,000s more do same

Sample Essay — Disagree

Although facilities are important, if universities are given a choice, they should spend money donated to them by hiring famous lecturers. Doing that would dramatically increase the quality of the schools. Accordingly, I disagree with the statement.

Universities must stress education, and there is no better way to do that than by employing famous professors. For one

thing, most famous lecturers are well known because they are good at teaching, so they will be able to impart a great amount of knowledge on their students. For another thing, students taking classes with famous lecturers will be more likely to pay attention during class, which will enable them to learn more. My older sister took a class with a famous history teacher once, and she still talks about how much she learned from him.

Something else to consider is that when universities hire famous professors, the best students will be eager to apply to those schools to study with those instructors. My brother is a senior in high school and is considering which school to attend. He hopes to major in engineering, and his grades are excellent, so he should get accepted at most of the schools he applies to. He is busy conducting research on the professors that teach in the engineering departments at certain schools in the country. He states that he only wants to attend a school with famous instructors since he knows he will get a top-notch education from them.

Last, when students study with famous lecturers, they are more likely to remember their university years fondly. As a result, when schools request donations from alumni, those former students will most likely donate money. These funds, in turn, can be used to improve the facilities at the schools. My sister always gives money when her university requests a donation. She does not give much, but she is one of thousands of alumni at her school. If many alumni feel the same way about the university as my sister, then her school can raise lots of money through donations, which can be used to improve the school.

I disagree with the statement because universities ought to spend money they receive as donations on hiring famous lecturers. The lecturers can teach students well and will attract outstanding students. Later, those students that graduate will probably donate to their former universities, which can use those funds on their facilities.

Chapter **10**

B | Outlining   p. 155

Sample Outline — Agree

Thesis Statement
If a person has the opportunity to go on a trip, that individual ought to do that instead of merely saving the money to use in the future.

First Supporting Idea
Topic Sentence:
- A trip can be a learning experience.

Supporting Example(s):

- can be learning experience
- went to Europe w/family → saw historical places, museums, & galleries
- was trip of lifetime → better than saving $ in bank

Second Supporting Idea

Topic Sentence:

- A trip can help people relax and get rid of their stress.

Supporting Example(s):

- can relax and get rid of stress
- parents have stressful jobs so take 2+ trips each year
- when start trip, parents look tired → when go home, parents look better

Third Supporting Idea

Topic Sentence:

- You never know what will happen in the future, so you should enjoy the present.

Supporting Example(s):

- should enjoy the present
- grandparents always saved → never traveled
- said would take trip someday → died before could do that

Conclusion

A person should take a trip rather than save money to use later.

C | Completing the Essay

p. 156

Sample Essay — Agree

If a person has the opportunity to go on a trip, that individual ought to do that instead of merely saving the money to use in the future. There are several reasons why I agree with the statement.

The first reason is that a trip can be a learning experience. My father received a bonus at his job last year, so my family traveled to Europe for two weeks. During that time, we visited many sites of historical interest, museums, and art galleries. I saw in person many places and things which I had previously read about in books. It was the trip of a lifetime and was a much better use of money than putting it in the bank to spend later.

The second reason is that a trip can help people relax and get rid of their stress. My parents work, and their jobs are quite stressful, so they make sure we take at least two trips every year. We normally go somewhere relaxing, such as the beach, and we stay for around a week or ten days. It is amazing how much my parents change during that time. When we start our trip, they look tired and stressed out, but when we return home, they look fresh and relaxed.

The third reason is that you never know what will happen in the future, so you should enjoy the present. My grandparents constantly saved for the future, so they rarely spent any money and never went anywhere. They refused to visit us at our home because they said they could not afford to travel. We had to go to their home in order to see them. They always said that they would have enough money to take a trip someday, but, sadly, they passed away before they ever went on one. I think they would have been much happier if they had worried less about saving money and taken a trip so that they could have enjoyed their lives more.

I fully agree with the statement. A person should take a trip rather than save money to use later. By taking a trip, a person can learn very much, get rid of stress, and enjoy the present rather than worry about the future.

Sample Essay — Disagree

While taking a trip can be fun, I disagree with the statement. I believe the opposite and think that people should save their money to use later rather than spend their money by going on a trip.

These days, too many people focus solely on the present and rarely consider the future. Those individuals really need to prepare for the future by depositing money in the bank and saving it for later. I love traveling with my family, but I understand when my parents announce that we cannot take a vacation because they want to save money. My parents recently said we will not travel anywhere this year because they are saving money for my college education. I would love to take a trip, but my parents are doing the right thing by saving for my future.

In addition, too many people waste money when they go on trips, so they would be better off saving their money instead. When people travel, they have a tendency to stay at expensive hotels, to dine at five-star restaurants, and to buy souvenirs that they do not need. One of my friends recently returned from a trip. When he told me about it, I was shocked. His family flew in first class, stayed at a beachside resort, and ate expensive meals every day. My friend's family is not wealthy either. They should have stayed home and saved that money rather than being so wasteful.

Something else to consider is that you never know what will happen in the future, so it is prudent to save money. Last year, my parents decided not to travel but to save the bonuses they had earned at their jobs. That was a wise decision because the family car broke down a couple of weeks later. They had to buy a brand-new car, which they would not have been able to afford if we had gone on a trip. Thanks to smart planning for the future, my family did not experience any financial problems.

I disagree with the statement because I believe it is better to save money for the future than to take a trip. People ought to focus on the future and be prepared for sudden problems that might arise, and they also waste money on trips, so they ought to stay home and save their money.

Sample Outline — Agree

1 are winners and losers
- in sports, people win and lose games
- don't always win and don't always lose → just like in life

2 teamwork is necessary
- individual skills aren't important → how work well as team is important
- father's team members are skilled → have bad teamwork so have trouble w/projects

3 life is unfair
- lost basketball game from bad call by ref → unfair to lose
- coach said life is unfair → sometimes unfair things happen

Sample Essay — Agree

I completely agree with the statement. There are numerous important lessons about life that people can learn by playing sports. I shall write about three of them.

The first lesson is that there are winners and losers. When a person plays a sport, there will be a winner and a loser. The same thing is true in life. Of course, just like in sports, merely because a person wins once does not mean that individual will win all the time. The same is true about losing as a person may lose once but win later. This is exactly what happens with my basketball team: Sometimes we win games, and sometimes we lose games.

The second lesson is that teamwork is frequently necessary to do something well. I play on a basketball team and have learned that it does not matter how good each individual player is. What matters is how well those players work together as a team. Recently, I heard my father talking about his job. He has some outstanding employees on his team, but they get along poorly with one another. As a result, they have a hard time completing projects because they have terrible teamwork. When my father mentioned that, I realized they could have learned about teamwork by playing sports.

The third lesson is that life, just like sports, is unfair. Last week, my basketball team was playing a game. In the final seconds, the referee called a foul on one of my teammates even though he was nowhere near the ball. Because of that foul, we lost the game. It was unfair that the referee was biased in favor of the opposing team. After the game ended, our coach said it was not right that we had lost, but he also mentioned that life is not fair. He told us that sometimes there will be injustices, so it is not a bad thing that we experience an incident of unfairness now.

There are so many lessons that sports can teach people about life. Three are that people can learn there are winners and losers, teamwork is important, and life is unfair. If more people played sports, they could learn about these life lessons at an early age.

Sample Outline — Disagree

1 play sports for fun
- play w/friends → don't take games seriously
- don't keep score → just like playing and having fun

2 want to stay in good shape
- many people out of shape → can be in shape by playing sports
- want to lose weight → doesn't relate to life lessons

3 don't think about sports when playing
- no strategy → don't worry about winning or losing
- just want to play game → forget about game when finishes and go home

Sample Essay — Disagree

I have heard people declare that there are many life lessons to be learned from sports, but I disagree with them. In fact, I do not believe that people can learn about life by playing sports.

I play sports with my friends all the time, but I only participate in them for fun. My friends and I enjoy playing soccer, basketball, baseball, and other sports after school and on the weekend. We do not take any of the games seriously though. In most cases, we do not even bother to keep score. We simply like playing games and having fun with one another.

Another reason we play sports is that we are interested in staying in good shape. These days, it is easy to become overweight and to get out of shape. Many people my age spend most of their time indoors watching television or using computers, and they also consume large amounts of junk food. I used to be like that, but I decided to get in shape, so I began playing sports. For me, one of the primary objectives of sports is to lose weight so that I can be healthy and in excellent physical condition. I do not see how that relates to any life lessons.

When I play sports, I do not think about anything but just focus on whatever sport it is I am playing. I do not concern myself with strategy, nor do I worry about whether or not I am going to win the game or if the referee is being fair. I have heard people claim that those are important life lessons, but they are of no concern to me or any of the other people with whom I play sports. We merely go out on the playing field, kick or hit the ball around, and have a good time. When the game is over, we forget about it and go home.

I do not understand how people can think that there are life lessons to be learned from playing sports. I participate in sports, but I only do them to have fun and to lose weight, and I do not give them much thought while I am playing them. For those reasons, I disagree with the statement.

TASK 1 | Integrated Writing Task p. 163

Listening Script

Now listen to part of a lecture on the topic you just read about.

M Professor: Nowadays, businesses are devising health incentive plans for their employees. Basically, uh, the companies are rewarding their workers for getting into shape, stopping bad habits, and being healthy in general. You might consider these plans positive features, but they're actually rather controversial. Let me explain why . . .

One problem is that these plans are often effective for short periods of time but fail the longer they go on. Why's that . . . ? Well, people may visit health clubs, stop smoking, or give up their favorite junk foods for a while, but let's be honest . . . It's hard to quit those activities for years. In fact, it's virtually inevitable that most people will resume their bad habits at some point in their lives. And when employees return to their old ways, they frequently get discouraged and depressed, which is neither good for them nor their employers.

Numerous employees decry these plans as unfair if they compensate workers who are already healthy since those people get rewarded for doing nothing. Some people have trouble staying healthy due to, uh, a lack of time or family obligations, and there's growing evidence that genes cause some people to be overweight. On the other hand, healthy people claim it's unfair for them to miss out on rewards being given to people they consider lazy and lacking in self-control.

What about companies . . . ? They institute these programs to increase productivity and to save money by having their employees take fewer sick days. But remember that people don't always take sick days because they're sick. They might, um, have family commitments, have a sick spouse or child, or simply be too tired to work that day and need a break. So I imagine that no matter what programs exist, people will still end up taking the same number of sick days as before.

Sample Essay

In his lecture, the professor discusses health incentive plans that some businesses use to encourage their employees to become healthier. He is skeptical of their effectiveness and casts doubt on the arguments in their favor that are mentioned in the reading passage.

The professor begins by remarking that these plans are usually only effective for short periods of time. He says that people can stop their bad habits for a while but eventually resume them, which makes them disappointed and sad. In mentioning those facts, the professor disregards the argument in the reading passage that these programs encourage employees to get healthier.

The next argument the professor takes on concerns who gets rewarded. While the reading passage mentions that incentives given to employees make them want to get in shape, the professor points out a problem with who gets the incentives. Some employees do not want healthy individuals to get rewards since they are already in shape whereas healthy employees do not want lazy employees to be rewarded for their lack of self-control.

The final point covered concerns companies themselves. The author of the reading passage believes companies will save money and become more profitable with these programs. But the professor comments that employees take sick days for reasons other than illnesses, so they will probably continue acting the same way in the future.

TASK 2 | Independent Writing Task p. 168

Sample Essay — Agree

I strongly agree with the statement. In my opinion, both schools and businesses should have rules regarding the types of clothing that people are allowed to wear at them. I feel this way for three main reasons.

First, it is crucial that everyone at a school or business look similar to foster a sense of togetherness. I wear a uniform at my school, and I like it when I see my fellow students wearing the same outfit. It makes me feel like we are members of the same team. This is especially true when I am off campus. Whenever I see another student with my school's uniform on, I always say hi even if I do not personally know that particular student. Because we belong to the same school, we have a connection with each other.

Second, when everyone at a school or business wears similar or identical clothes, it looks more professional. I have seen group pictures of students at schools with no uniforms, and they do not look nearly as good as the group pictures of students wearing uniforms. In addition, I love visiting my mother's place of business. All the employees wear similar clothes since her company has regulations regarding that, so everyone there looks very professional. I think it must be a great place to work.

Third, when a school or business has rules regarding the types of clothes people can wear, it reduces the amount of competition between the students or employees. My sister attends a school with no dress code, so the students there waste tons of money on clothes. They always try to outdo one another with regard to who can wear the most expensive or stylish clothes, which seems like a huge waste of time and money to me. If those students had to wear uniforms, they could quit focusing on clothes and start thinking more about their schoolwork.

I believe schools and businesses should regulate how people dress because it can unite people, it looks more professional, and it can reduce competition between others. For those three reasons, I agree with the statement.

Sample Essay — Disagree

There are many students and businesspeople who support schools and businesses having dress codes or making people wear uniforms. I, however, am not one of those individuals, so I disagree with the statement.

For starters, making people dress similarly or the same stifles creativity. Several of my friends have their own unique styles when they are not at school, but they have to wear uniforms when they go to class, which prevents them from showing off their uniqueness. I can see how unhappy they look when they put their uniforms on and blend in with all the other students. Once they return home, however, they change out of their uniforms and put their regular clothes back on. At that time, they can be creative in their styles and resume being happy.

Something else to consider is that people feel comfortable in different types of clothes. Personally, I do not mind wearing a school uniform, but my brother despises his. He has to wear a coat and tie to school every day, but he hates wearing ties. He remarks that he feels like his tie is choking him, so he constantly tugs at it. He would be much more comfortable in a T-shirt and shorts, but his school does not permit him to wear casual clothes like those.

Finally, clothes are really not important. What is important is how well the people wearing the clothes perform. My father is an outstanding salesman at his company, so his manager does not care what my father wears to work. The only thing his boss cares about is how many sales my father makes each day. The same is true for my mother, who is a chef at a restaurant. The owner of the restaurant does not bother my mother about her clothes because he wants her to make the most delicious meals possible, not look stylish. For each of my parents, their job performances, not their clothes, are important.

I disagree with the statement because I do not believe schools or businesses should tell people what to wear. Having a dress code can reduce people's creativity, uniforms are often uncomfortable, and clothes are not particularly important. Those three reasons explain exactly why I believe the statement is wrong.